LOCOMOTION PAPERS

Rails to Achill

A West of Ireland Branch Line

by
Jonathan Beaumont

'Tiocfaidh an lá nuair a thabharfaidh carráiste tine ar rothaí iarainn bás'

'The day will come when fire carriages on iron wheels will bring death'

Brian Rua O Cearbhain
Ennis, 17th Century

THE OAKWOOD PRESS

© Oakwood Press & Jonathan Beaumont 2002

British Library Cataloguing in Publication Data
A Record for this book is available from the British Library
ISBN 0 85361 588 8

Typeset by Oakwood Graphics.
Repro by Ford Graphics, Ringwood, Hants.
Printed by Inkon Printers Ltd, Yateley, Hants.

Dedication

To my parents, Elsie and Henry, whose choice of annual holiday first introduced me to the remains of the Achill line at Mallaranny in the 1960s, and my wife Maureen and family, for their forbearance while I shut myself into the study, and disappeared for days on end in order to carry out research.

Rear cover, top: Railway Clearing House map showing the line to Achill.

Rear cover, bottom: A previously unpublished postcard of the Irish Industrial Minerals Co. line and locomotives on Achill Island.   *The late D. Farrar*

Published by The Oakwood Press (Usk), P.O. Box 13, Usk, Mon., NP15 1YS.
E-mail: oakwood-press@dial.pipex.com
Website: www.oakwood-press.dial.pipex.com

Contents

No. 530, formerly No. 36 *Empress of Austria*, at Westport in the early 1930s. This locomotive was built by Beyer, Peacock & Co. of Manchester in 1881 as a 2-4-0, and rebuilt by the Midland Great Western Railway in 1900 as a 4-4-0 for use on the Achill line. This engine was in use after the line closed until 1949, when she was scrapped in Dublin. In this picture, the locomotive still carries its original MGWR pattern chimney - a few years later, this had been replaced by a standard Inchicore design. *Ernie Shepherd*

Achill Island from the mainland. In the distance, Achill Sound village can be seen on the left. This is where the railway ended, and a road bridge connects the island with the road to Westport. This gives an idea of the unspoilt scenery to be seen in the area.   *Author*

A scene near Mulrany (Mallaranny in railway parlance) showing the spectacular scenery the line traversed. The railway track was on the high embankment to the right of the picture, above Bellacragher Bay. In railway days, this bank taxed the abilities of locomotive crews, as it approached the station on a curve, and with a 1 in 70 gradient for over a mile. One afternoon in 1897, shots were fired at an Achill-bound train as it passed near here. Nobody was ever brought to account for this sinister incident. In July 1905, a train became derailed close by as a result of excess speed.   *Author*

Introduction

If you travel from Westport in the west of Ireland through Newport and Mulrany to Achill Sound today, here and there you will see overgrown sections of railway embankment, bridges and a couple of tunnels, as well as the magnificent stone viaduct across the river in Newport. These are the surviving remnants of the old Achill line - a branch line built at the close of the 19th century to help develop the area and link it with the outside world.

The promoters of the line had high hopes for its future, and the railway was opened to the public in several sections in 1894/5. It proved to be a great social and economic asset to this area of County Mayo, but traffic never consistently reached the levels originally anticipated, and as a result the line was not profitable for much of the year. Development of road traffic in the 1930s sealed the fate of the rails to Achill, and the last train ran in the autumn of 1937 - a mere 42 years after the line had opened. Since then, trains have operated from Dublin just as far as Westport, which is now the railhead for the area. The track onwards to Achill was dismantled in 1938.

Today, the remaining stone and earthworks, along with the old railway station buildings at Newport, Mulrany and Achill Sound stand in mute testimony to the line; the local businessmen who promoted it, the builders, and the people who used it. The course of the line is still very identifiable for most of its length, despite over 60 years having elapsed since the last train ran. Here and there, parts of it have a new use now. The viaduct in Newport is a beautifully restored prominent local landmark with a path along the top, giving the visitor a glimpse of the spectacular views that were possible from the train. Newport goods shed is now a small chapel, while Achill station has become a guesthouse.

This is the story of the 'Achill Railway' - described by travellers at the turn of the 20th century as 'one of the most scenic railway journeys in these Islands'.

Newport Viaduct. The station was immediately beyond this impressive structure on the left, where the white roof of a car showroom is currently visible. The viaduct is now a public walkway, from which a fine view of the area may be had. *Author*

Chapter One

Setting the Scene

Railway construction in Ireland commenced in the 1830s, and the first public line was opened between Dublin and Dun Laoghaire (then known as Kingstown) in 1834. During the next 30 years, main lines spread across the country to the extent that all major centres in Ireland were rail-connected. Gradually, smaller towns and villages joined the system, often connected by small local railway companies, many of which were later absorbed into the bigger ones.

The West of Ireland was no exception. The Midland Great Western Railway (MGWR) operated the first train from Dublin to Galway in 1851. Plans followed to connect Mayo and Roscommon with this line and between 1860 and 1865 the Great Northern & Western Railway was opened for traffic in stages, eventually connecting Athlone (on the MGWR line) with Westport. The first train arrived in Westport on 29th January, 1865. By 1873, Ballina had been connected to the railway system as well, and many schemes were being proposed for further extensions in west Mayo.

Little notice was taken at this stage of Achill - most of the proposals involved lines directed towards Belmullet, either via Ballycastle on the north coast of Mayo, or a more direct route via Crossmolina. These proposals were largely influenced by other plans to develop Belmullet as a transatlantic port: plans that needless to say never came into being. Achill was a remote community at this time, reached only by boat from the mainland - a road bridge connecting the island to the mainland was not built until 1887.

In 1889, railway building in Ireland entered a new stage with the passage of the Light Railways (Ireland) Act. This Act of Parliament made possible the construction of railway lines in comparatively remote areas where normal commercial interests might have been less enthusiastic about building them. Promoted largely by Arthur Balfour, Chief Secretary for Ireland, the Act introduced Government grants for such lines, and promotional procedures were made easier. In 1890, the Tramways Act allowed the promoter of a new line to transfer their powers to an existing company. In Mayo, this would enable the promoter of any of the proposed lines to have the line built and operated by the MGWR.

Elsewhere in Ireland, a number of lines were built under these initiatives, mostly in the West. Many were constructed to the narrow 3 ft gauge, instead of the Irish standard 5 ft 3 in. gauge. For every line built, many more were proposed, some of the schemes being totally unrealistic, and Mayo was no exception.

Following the 'Balfour Act' as it became known, a rush of optimism seems to have carried many local businessmen, and not a few clergy, towards suggesting two possible lines to Belmullet from Ballina, one from Castlebar to Newport, one from Westport via Newport to Belmullet, and another from Castlebar to Belmullet via Newport. The latter two, if built, would have overlapped in part the eventual route of the Achill line, but all these proposals came to nothing. (One further scheme involved extending the existing railway to Ballina as far as Killala, some eight miles to the north. This line was approved, and opened in 1893.)

In the meantime, business interests in Newport and Achill had made representations to the Board of the Midland Great Western Railway, which had taken over the Great Northern & Western in 1890. In view of this, and the fact that one of the proposed Belmullet routes would have passed through Newport and Mallaranny*, approval was given by a Government Commission for a line to be built from Westport to Mallaranny via Newport. It was hoped that this would form a compromise - a railway beyond Newport but less than halfway from Westport to Belmullet! The Midland Great Western watched with interest, but stepped back from frequent invitations for more direct involvement. By 1890, the MGWR had formulated a broad policy that they would operate a line built to their standards by another promoter, or the Government; and they would be willing to build a line themselves provided that substantial funding for the construction came from elsewhere. Given the economic nature of the areas involved, this was hardly surprising. Even at that stage, it is evident that reservations were held by the MGWR's Board about the viability of many such lines.

The Public Works Commission had reported on a proposed 'West Mayo Light Railway' in March 1890. This railway to Mallaranny was initially planned as a steam tramway, following the road for much of its length. Future plans would include the possibility of extension in the Belmullet direction, at least as far as Claggan pier, some miles to the north of Mallaranny. It was suggested that it would be most economical to build the line to the 3 ft narrow gauge. But support from the MGWR was essential for the most economic working of any new line in the area, and that company stipulated that it would only be prepared to enter into a working arrangement if the line was constructed to the standard 5 ft 3 in. gauge. The MGWR was asked if it would cover the cost difference between building the line to narrow gauge and to broad gauge, but it refused, saying that this would not be in its shareholder's interests. The junction with the main line at Westport was originally planned to be via a 'back shunt' - presumably an arrangement such as that at Galway, where the Clifden line started. The only other information recorded is that it was felt that an end-on junction with the main line, allowing through running, would be preferable. This change involved an unspecified 'deviation half a mile in length' from the first plan.

The Board of the MGWR held an Extraordinary General Meeting in 1890 to consider the 'Balfour Lines' proposed - Ballina to Killala as well as Westport to Mallaranny. It was reported in July 1890 that the Midland's Engineer was already plotting out the proposed route of the Mallaranny line, and that new sidings were to be installed at Westport to accommodate construction trains for the line. The Engineer pointed out a number of objections to the plan for a roadside steam tramway, mostly concerning steep gradients.

By the autumn of 1890, the MGWR's Chairman had submitted proposals to the Government for an agreement regarding construction, operation and

---

* Mulrany was then known as Mallaranny, and throughout the life of the railway this spelling was used by the railway companies.

maintenance of proposed railways from Westport to 'Mullaranny'; Ballina to Killala, and Galway to Clifden. The Board of Works held a public inquiry in October 1890, following which the plans were altered by reducing the number of level crossings on the line, and moving the route away from the roadside onto its own right of way.

In August 1890 a meeting took place between Sir Ralph Cusack, the MGWR's Chairman, and the Chief Secretary for Ireland, following which an agreement to build the Westport-Mallaranny line was drawn up. But this was the easy bit: much wrangling between the Government, the MGWR, the builders and others was to follow over the next few years!

Balfour himself visited the area in the autumn. The Parish Priest at Achill, Father John Connolly, and a deputation of Achill businessmen laid on an impressive reception for him. The story is told that, in contrast, nobody met him officially when he visited Belmullet due to interference from people there who had interests in road transport. As a result, Balfour is said to have been more impressed with the case put to him at Achill Sound, where he told a large crowd of islanders that the railway would be a 'boon that will not pass with the passing year, but will last for you and your children for ever'. In any event, the merits of developing the fledgling tourist industry in that area and the benefits to the fishing industry were emphasised. It was also argued that Achill was a deprived area still reeling after the effects of the Great Famine - though it was by no means the only district in such difficulties. The decision to extend the railway from Mallaranny to Achill was taken soon afterwards and a survey of the proposed line commenced.

Westport station on a sunny afternoon in the mid-1930s. A passenger chats with the driver of No. 535 on an Achill-bound train awaiting departure. The station has changed little between then and now. *C.P. Friel Collection*

Chapter Two

Building the Railway:
Westport to Mallaranny

The potato harvest had failed badly over the winter of 1890/1891 in many areas of the West. While not as severe overall as the worst Famine years of the middle of the century, Co. Mayo was among the hardest hit this time round. The Government was therefore anxious to have the work started without delay to provide employment, and a contract was drawn up immediately to start the work, in advance of proper tenders being submitted and suitable contractors chosen. The contractor who started this work off was Robert Worthington of Dublin. Worthington was awarded both the Westport-Mallaranny and Mallaranny-Achill contracts and work commenced either side of Newport and at Achill Sound itself, where the first sod was turned without ceremony on 4th December, 1890. The Royal Irish Constabulary kept statistics for the Government on how effective this work was as unemployment relief, and we can therefore tell that over Christmas 1890 over a thousand local men were employed at Newport, Knocklougha, Mallaranny and Achill Sound. The men were paid at the following weekly rates:

Gangers	16	shillings
Labourers	12	shillings
'Boys '	6-10	shillings

By March 1891, a total of 1,313 men were employed on both the Westport-Mallaranny and Mallaranny-Achill temporary contracts.

In the meantime, tenders were being invited for the principal contracts. Worthington was of course one; five other contractors were invited to submit theirs, though two eventually withdrew 'for want of information '. Eventually, firm quotations were received from the following four.

R. Worthington	£110,000
T.H. Falkiner	£115,000
McCrea & McFarland	£105,346
Collen Bros	£125,000

McCrea & McFarland soon withdrew their offer due to a miscalculation they had made. Worthington's price was quoted on condition that he was also granted the contract to build the Galway-Clifden branch, which was in the same stage of planning further south. This was approved. Throughout 1891, much correspondence was exchanged between Worthington, his engineer (W. Barrington of Limerick), the MGWR and officials of Government bodies - suffice to say that all the necessary paperwork was completed and statutory conditions were complied with.

But all was not well with the construction gangs. Workers at Westport and Newport went on strike for higher pay in the early months of 1891. Their employment was discontinued and replacements were found. A foretaste of future friction between the MGWR, Worthington and Barrington appeared in the form of a complaint from the latter to the MGWR that not enough land had been given to the contractor for the construction of three cuttings and an embankment between Westport and Mallaranny. The MGWR asked its solicitor to investigate. His reply is not recorded!

Barrington also told the MGWR that alterations to the plans were necessary in the townland of Clooneen, between Westport and Newport, on land owned by a B. Mulloy. A station was planned at Doontrusk, though this was never actually built.

Worthington then recommended to the MGWR that the proposed tunnel at Barley Hill, between Westport and Newport, should be replaced with a deep cutting. The company refused to agree to this, as its Chief Engineer, Mr Purcell O'Neill, had stated that a cutting at that point would be likely to subside due to the nature of the soil. Instead, Worthington was told he could shorten the tunnel by 100 ft. He planned to line the inside of the tunnel with brick on the roof and masonry on the sides - a cost-cutting measure, apparently, being different from the original plan. Any alterations to this tunnel were to be carried out at Worthington's expense.

In December 1891, the MGWR changed its mind and Worthington was told he could substitute a cutting for the tunnel if necessary. This was done - but not before further wrangling between contractor and railway company regarding the quality of the rubble masonry used to line the interior.

At Kilbride, just south of Newport, a similar situation arose, and in fact two alternative routes for the line were actually built - one going around the side of the hill, and one through it via a deep cutting and tunnel. Track was laid at some stage along both, although the route through the tunnel appears to have been used from the outset. As late as the 1970s it was just possible to make out the imprints of sleepers on the trackbed of the 'deviation ' around the hill - indicating the presence of track there at one time. Marks like this may remain in undisturbed ground for years, and it is possible that a temporary line was laid here at the time of construction, perhaps remaining in a derelict state for many years afterwards.

Tenders were now invited to supply track materials. Five firms sought the contract to ship 7,000 tons of rails in from England, while six firms offered to provide the appropriate quantity of 'half-round' sleepers.

Further heated discussion and dispute took place - the construction of the bridge over Castlebar Street in Newport was met with opposition by the townspeople who said it was inconveniently located. After the usual flurry of exchanges, it was agreed to put a footpath under it.

During construction, the MGWR was submitting regular claims to the Board of Works (BoW) for reimbursement of the sums paid out in connection with the line's construction. In November 1891, the company overpaid the contractors by £1,087, and claimed this from the BoW, who refused to refund it. The company justified its claim by saying that this was what Worthington had invoiced it for, and it seems that this explanation was sufficient, since no further mention was made of it. But financial matters continued to cause problems, with Worthington complaining to the MGWR in February 1892 that Barrington was

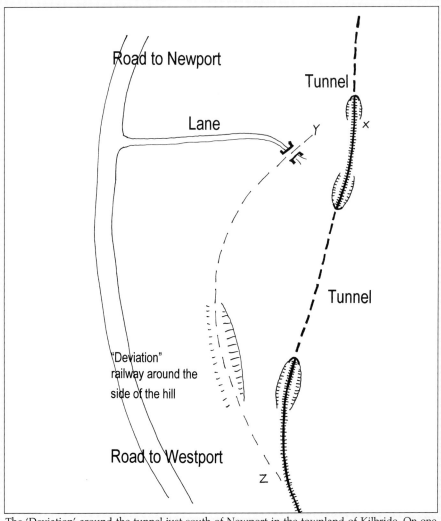

The 'Deviation' around the tunnel just south of Newport in the townland of Kilbride. On one copy of the original Engineer's drawings, this line (Z-X) is pencilled in, but no other clear reference is made to the line. The line was built in part, and the remains of it could be seen until the early 1970s. As shown, it left the main line just south of the tunnels and curved up around the side of the hill, before ending at 'Y' on the plan. At this point, the trackbed was about one and a half metres above the level of the main line, so that the logical connection between Y and X could never have been completed. It is clear that track was laid on the section between Y and Z, as the marks where the sleepers had been were visible on the ground 30 years after the line had closed. The purpose of this short line is unclear. If the track had been connected to the main line at Z, it could have been used as a siding to store cattle wagons on fair days at Newport, but some reference to it would surely survive in traffic notices or Working Time Tables. No surviving company records make any reference to a siding here at all. A more likely possibility is that while the line was being built, and there was some controversy over whether a tunnel or cutting was to be built at this point, some track was laid down. This could have remained undisturbed, but unconnected with the running line, for years afterwards. Such a section of track may even have been a remnant of a temporary line used by the line's builders. Had this occurred, little effort would have been made to recover such a short stretch of track and when it was eventually taken away, the imprint of the sleepers on the ground would have remained.

The 'Deviation', Kilbride, Newport. This small bridge is all that survives: it carries a farm track under the trackbed. It is unclear whether track was ever laid over the bridge - if it was, no use seems to have been made of it. *Author*

P L A N S.

THE AREAS MARKED ON PLANS ARE IN STATUTE MEASURE.
SCALE 200 FEET TO 1 INCH.

NOTE.--*The quantities are figured in Cubic Yards,*
The heights in feet and decimals of a foot.

Scales, $\left\{ \begin{array}{l} \textit{Horizontal 200 feet to 1 inch.} \\ \textit{Vertical 20 feet to 1 inch.} \end{array} \right.$

not passing on payments to him, resulting in delays in construction. The MGWR promised to put pressure on Barrington to be more prompt. However, over the next year or more, the same complaint was made repeatedly by Worthington.

A number of other alterations to culverts, minor level crossings, cuttings and bridges were approved during this stage of construction. Few are of note, though much correspondence was exchanged regarding diversion of the public road at Burrishoole: the local landowner there wanted the company to pay for alterations to his gates, not an unreasonable request. Eventually this matter was resolved amicably.

In July 1892 the contractors realised they were running out of time, since the original contract said that the line to Mallaranny was to be ready by December that year. An extension of 18 months was granted.

The tunnel at Newport was the subject of the next exchange. The MGWR told Barrington that they wanted him to have a 'resident engineer ' living in Newport to provide constant supervision of the construction of the tunnel. The impression is given that the MGWR was worried about accidents taking place on the site when not supervised, presumably at times of the day or week when work was not in progress. Barrington appears to have been irritated by this request, insisting that his existing arrangements were adequate, and telling the MGWR that there was no suitable house in Newport for an engineer to live in anyway! He added that the proposed site for the station at Newport (believed to have been to the east of the river) was 'most objectionable', claiming that suitable flat land was available 'half a furlong further along'. The company gave this last point speedy consideration and Barrington was asked not to proceed with the original station. It must be assumed that the land Barrington referred to was at the location of the station building where it now stands. But Barrington still refused to appoint a 'Masonry Inspector' to supervise the tunnel, repeating that his own men could keep adequate watch. By this time, the company was occupied with the final stages of planning the work on the Achill extension, and further correspondence of this nature must have been unwelcome, to say the least. But Barrington came back to the MGWR in April 1892 complaining that he had been underpaid, and that alterations to a bridge at Westport were to cost £400 extra. The MGWR refused to pay him further, as the company's Engineer, O'Neill stated that Barrington 'has been largely overpaid already'. O'Neill disputed the figure of £400 for the bridge, and continued by disagreeing with Barrington over the drawings for the viaduct across the river in Newport!

With the constant bickering between the two unresolved, both parties wrote to the MGWR Board for guidance. The issue of the masonry inspector in the tunnel arose again, and Barrington maintained that the appointment of such a person 'has nothing whatsoever to do with the Engineering Supervision ' (undertaken by him, presumably). He now claimed that he had had an interview with the Chairman of the MGWR to the effect that the MGWR would appoint and pay for an inspector (exact duties not defined). He said he would be prepared to meet half this cost. However, the matter seems to have ceased to worry the MGWR after this, as no specific appointment is recorded as having been made.

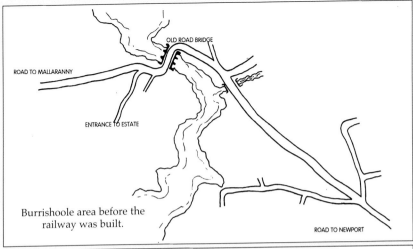

Burrishoole area before the railway was built.

ROAD TO MALLARANNY

OLD ROAD BRIDGE

ENTRANCE TO ESTATE

ROAD TO NEWPORT

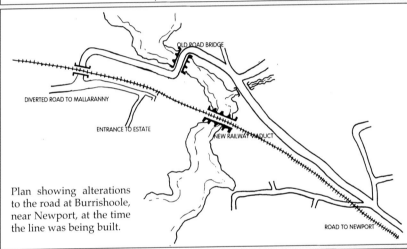

Plan showing alterations to the road at Burrishoole, near Newport, at the time the line was being built.

OLD ROAD BRIDGE

DIVERTED ROAD TO MALLARANNY

ENTRANCE TO ESTATE

NEW RAILWAY VIADUCT

ROAD TO NEWPORT

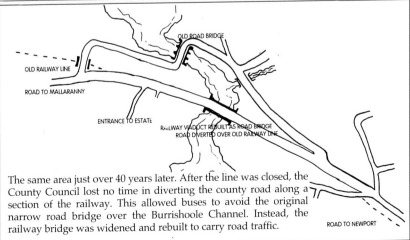

The same area just over 40 years later. After the line was closed, the County Council lost no time in diverting the county road along a section of the railway. This allowed buses to avoid the original narrow road bridge over the Burrishoole Channel. Instead, the railway bridge was widened and rebuilt to carry road traffic.

OLD RAILWAY LINE

OLD ROAD BRIDGE

ROAD TO MALLARANNY

ENTRANCE TO ESTATE

RAILWAY VIADUCT REBUILT AS ROAD BRIDGE
ROAD DIVERTED OVER OLD RAILWAY LINE

ROAD TO NEWPORT

Burrishoole, near Newport. The old road to Achill was carried over the southern end of Furnace Lough by this narrow bridge (*above*). Small wonder that the prospect of buses replacing trains caused consternation for the local authority! The solution was to divert the road over the railway for a short stretch. The railway viaduct was demolished down to pier level, and a new bridge built over the top of it (*below*). The old railway retaining walls survive as part of the road structure.
(Both) Author

Entrance to tunnel at Newport, with track maintenance gang present, soon after the line opened. The earth surrounds to the tunnel look somewhat unstable, and the fencing appears to be roughly finished. Several instances were recorded at the time of rocks rolling down to track level. No doubt the eventual cover of grass and weeds stabilised the ground.

Lawrence Collection, courtesy National Library of Ireland

Newport viaduct, looking towards the tunnel and the Westport direction. Note the signal controlling train entry to the station, which was immediately to the left of the picture.

Lawrence Collection, courtesy National Library of Ireland

Worthington then entered the fray, complaining to the MGWR that Barrington was 'unbusinesslike and irregular' in dealing with Construction Certificates and payments. This was denied, both parties blaming each other for lack of communication in day to day dealings. Worthington claimed Barrington had not given him some of the plans. Barrington said he had, then Worthington admitted he had found them, but that certain details were missing which prevented him from buying materials. The MGWR, as ever visualising delays in construction, told Barrington, rather sharply, to co-operate with Worthington. At this stage Barrington said he would comply.

But this peace did not last for long. Barrington complained that the payments the company made to him each month were not sufficient for him to pay Worthington, and he requested that an independent arbitrator (a Mr B.B. Stoney) be appointed under the terms of the agreement he had with the company. However O'Neill reported to the MGWR Board that payments to Barrington had been 'liberal', and the request was refused. Barrington repeatedly insisted he was not being paid enough, saying that inadequate payments were going to cause delays in building some of the stations, which would involve him in further expense, which he now warned he intended to claim from the company. But the MGWR sat tight, and nothing further was paid. When Barrington raised this matter again some months later, he was told that the station plans should not cause delays, and that the company absolved itself of all responsibility for any costs incurred by him as previously claimed.

Contemporary records at this stage record a litany of sniping, petty claims, counter claims and disputes of which the above are only some examples, between Barrington and the company's Engineer, O'Neill. In January 1893, as well as the usual arguments over payments, Barrington wrote to the Board saying he objected to the tone of letters to him from O'Neill. O'Neill produced a file of correspondence between the two, whereupon the Board wrote to Barrington to tell him that they thought that O'Neill's tone was perfectly justified considering his own, but that they could not approve of either. Again, all concerned were told to avoid recurrences.

By now, work was in an advanced stage on the Westport-Mallaranny section. On 29th and 30th July, 1892 the line was inspected by the MGWR's Captain Smyth and O'Neill. A number of small alterations were recommended and carried out, despite Worthington observing that one change involved altering work he had done exactly to the letter of the plans. Newport station building was enlarged at a cost of £580, while Worthington successfully tendered for the new goods yard and cattle loading bank there at a cost of £3,100. Discussions took place with the Post Office regarding provision of telegraph equipment, and with the Railway Signal Company for the supply and installation of signalling equipment. The MGWR's Manager gave details to the Post Office of the proposed train service over the line, to allow them to decide which trains they wanted mails to travel on.

Uncertainty surrounded the exact location of Mallaranny station, as proposals had still not been finalised about the extension beyond there to Achill. Plans existed to build the station as a terminus, and some work had already been done before it was definitely known that the line was not to end there. This was stopped pending final confirmation. The Board of Works undertook to reply to the company by 23rd May, 1893 as to whether they would approve the extension. A temporary wooden platform was planned initially, to allow train services to start when the time came.

The line as far as Mallaranny was now almost ready: the MGWR placed an order with Kitson's of Leeds for three new locomotives for the line. They were to be the same design as three already built for the company by Sharp, Stewart & Co, Manchester. The locomotives were classified as 'E' class, and these six along with another six subsequently built by Kitson were to be used on a number of newly opened rural branch lines. In addition to Achill, the 'E' class locomotives were destined for the lines to Clifden, Killala, Athboy and Kingscourt. A number of new carriages to standard MGWR designs of the period were under construction for general traffic all over the system: some of these would come to the Mallaranny line as well.

By May 1893, the Post Office had quoted £790 for installation of telegraphic equipment, including the provision of 'three speaking instruments'.

Worthington was involved at this stage in other railway construction projects as well as the Mallaranny and Achill contracts. Partly as a result of problems he encountered elsewhere, he found himself in severe financial difficulties, and he wrote to the company in August 1893 asking for a payment for the final alterations along the line. The company ignored both this and two other such requests, and then offered him £850. In September he filed for bankruptcy, but not before the MGWR had just paid him another £300. Separately, Barrington then complained that his most recent payment had been 'utterly insufficient' to meet his expenses. The Directors refused to pay him more, due to the quantity of work still remaining to be done.

Despite all this, the MGWR pressed on with plans to open the line for public traffic. In November 1893, statutory notice was given to the Board of Trade of its intention to open the section from Westport to Newport. But it is clear that much work was still outstanding: the Grand Jury of County Mayo wrote to the MGWR to point out that walls were required for public safety along the line between Westport and Burrishoole Bridge. For much (or all) of this length, if any fencing had been provided at all, it was of light posts and wire. The company's Engineer, O'Neill, estimated that it would cost £5,700 to remedy, but it was approved in view of the planned opening. However, by 1901 the remedial work had not been completed, as a Father O'Toole who lived adjacent to the line offered to replace the fencing adjacent to his property at his own expense, as it was of poor quality. Naturally, the railway company agreed!

On 2nd January, 1894 Major General Hutchinson from the Board of Works inspected the line as far as Newport. He reported that three level crossings were not yet authorised for use, but subject to this being done the BoW passed the line as being fit for public use. He also required handrails to be installed on some bridges, including Newport viaduct, and completion of the passenger shelter in Newport station. An altered section of the public road in the townland of Knockchottaun was unfenced, and at another point construction of the railway embankment had caused flood water to build up and a suitable outlet was needed. O'Neill reported that these matters would be attended to shortly.

A letter to the MGWR from R. Gardiner, surety for Worthington, declined to give consent to the opening of the line, but this was later withdrawn.

It was planned at this time to build a carriage shed suitable for holding 12 vehicles, but it was not mentioned where this was to be. Either Achill or Westport would be the logical locations, but while a shed was eventually built at Achill it was not of that size. In any event, it is difficult to imagine any reason for as many as 12 carriages needing to be stabled at Achill. No shed of these dimensions was ever built on the Achill line.

Opening to Newport

On 1st February, 1894, the first public trains ran as far as Newport. This took place with little ceremony in contrast to the great occasions made out of the openings of railways in other parts of the country. A few weeks later, a Mr Thomas Grady wrote to the company objecting to the opening of the line as far as Newport only, suggesting that it should not have been opened at all until the section from Newport to Mallaranny was ready as well! The MGWR answered this curious letter by saying that the station at Mallaranny was not yet finished due to uncertainty over the plans to build the line beyond there to Achill.

But while trains were now running to Newport, work continued to complete the next section. Since Worthington's bankruptcy, the Midland Great Western Railway had taken over the role of contractor, continuing to employ Worthington's engineers and workmen.

Barrington now contacted the MGWR asking for final payment, including an extra sum on account of 'works having been protracted'. The company replied that they would not release him from his contract to supervise the work until the Board of Trade had passed the line as far as Mallaranny. They also refused to pay more than the original contract price. Barrington told the company that he would do no further work, since the delays were not his fault, and requested arbitration over whether he was to be held liable for further supervision. The company replied that they would release him provided the BoW had no objection, but that no further payment would be made.

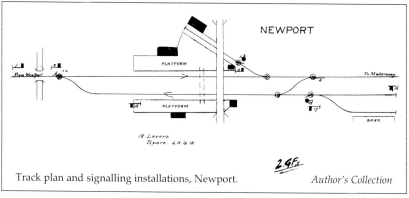

Track plan and signalling installations, Newport.   *Author's Collection*

Newport, approximately 1896/7. The newly built railway embankment in the foreground had yet to be covered by grass, while the station may be seen beyond the viaduct. Just visible in the background is an area surrounded by white fencing or walling - this was the cattle sidings area, of which no trace now remains. The railway continues beyond this in a cutting, towards Mallaranny.

Lawrence Collection, courtesy National Library of Ireland

The impression is sometimes given that the railway company was seen as a 'soft touch' by some of the professional people involved in consultancy work at this time. The Co. Mayo surveyor, E.K. Dixon, requested payment for attending the Board of Works inspection, which company declined.

One of the final pieces of work was the building of the water tower on the up platform at Mallaranny - the contract for this was given to Messrs Ross & Walpole, for payment of £88.

The building of the railway had given a great boost to employment in the area. As a result of the sacking of striking men at Newport in the early stages of the contract, a number of the workforce were from outside the immediate district, so that the benefits of the employment created were spread over a wider area. But the contract to build the line was nearing its end, and large numbers of labourers were being laid off. In January 1894 it was reported that only a small number of labourers were still employed, and these were men from outside the area. Comment was made in the House of Commons about their 'intemperate and quarrelsome' behaviour, which was causing considerable annoyance to the local people. No doubt the locals were looking forward to the day the last of them would leave.

A deputation of high-ranking officials from the MGWR, led by the Chairman Sir Ralph Cusack, the Secretary, and the locomotive engineer carried out a detailed inspection of the railway from Athlone-Westport and onwards to Achill, in May 1894. By this stage, work was under way on the Mallaranny to Achill section (as will be seen later), the line from Newport to Mallaranny was ready for opening, and the Westport-Newport section was fully operational. The inspecting party declared themselves satisfied with what they saw, so the MGWR gave the statutory one month's notice that they intended to open the line onwards from Newport to Mallaranny on 23rd June, 1894.

The Drowning Tragedy

But before the opening of this next section could officially take place, a terrible tragedy occurred, not immediately connected with the railway. There was a long standing practice in the West of Ireland for young men and women to travel to Britain for seasonal farming work. In the Achill/Corraun area, a large proportion of the young population set sail for Scotland every summer to work in the potato fields there. There was no port on Achill Island suitable for a large steamship to call, so these teenagers and young adults would walk the whole way from the island to Westport; or alternately sail in a hooker from the island to Westport to board the ship. On 14th June, 1894, over 400 young people, some as young as 12, boarded four hookers at Darby's Point, at the south end of Achill Island. They came from all districts on the island, as well as the western end of the Corraun peninsula. Some had been walking to Darby's Point since the previous day. They set sail for Westport as planned. As the heavily loaded hookers approached the harbour past Annagh Head the steamship due to set sail for Scotland came into view, moored in calm water just outside Westport. Many of the young people on the hookers had never seen such a sight before,

OF
YOUR CHARITY
PRAY FOR THE SOULS
OF

MARY MALLEY	MARY PATTEN
MAGGIE MALLEY	HONOR PATTEN
ANNIE MALLEY	BRIDG.T LYNCHEHAUN
JOSEPH WEIR	MARY.A LAVELLE
BRIDGET WEIR	SEBINA QUINN
BRIDGET M.LOUGHLIN	MARY SCANLON
PAT O DONNELL	BRIDGET JOYCE
MARG.T O DONNELL	MARY CAFFERKY
WINIFRED M.NEELA	MARY M.FARLAND
MRS. DOOGAN	MARY COONEY
MARTIN COONEY	THO.S CAFFERKEY
JOSEPH COONEY	PAT CAFFERKEY
NANCY COONEY	MRS MULLOY
CATHERINE WALSH	CATH.NE GALLAGHER
SEBINA M.NEELA	MARY PATTEN
JOHN PATTEN	HONOR ENGLISH

WHO WERE ACCIDENTALLY DROWNED
IN CLEW BAY
ON JUNE 14.TH 1894
R. I. P.

Commemorative headstone in Kildownet Old Cemetery, Achill Island. This was erected following the burial of the victims of the Clew Bay drowning tragedy, whose remains were taken by train to Achill. There is another headstone for the victims of the fire tragedy in 1937.

Author

and they clamoured to one side of the small boats to have a good look at the SS *Elm*. Some of their friends were already on board, presumably having arrived in Westport earlier. One hooker, the *Victory*, which was part owned by the Sweeney family of Achill Sound, and partly by John Healy (who was at the helm), capsized due to the sudden shift in its load. The other hookers, already overloaded, could only continue to Westport to discharge their own loads, before returning to try to rescue those in the sea. Many were rescued, but 32 people were drowned, ranging in age from 12 to 40. Arrangements had to made to have their remains transported back to Achill, and the MGWR was asked to help. A train was loaded at Westport Quay station, proceeding to the town station and onwards along the new line, on 16th June. The coffins of all but two victims were aboard - the other two had not yet been recovered from the sea. Eighty mourners travelled with the train, which left Westport at 10.30 am. Since the regular train service only operated as far as Newport and the line to Mallaranny had not yet been passed for traffic, once the carriages containing the coffins and mourners reached Newport they were coupled up to Worthington's own locomotive which had been used in the construction work. It is probable that this locomotive was an 0-6-0 saddle tank locomotive built by the Hunslet Engine Co., Leeds, in 1889, and resold to the Great Northern Railway in 1908. In Newport station, the father of a 16-year-old victim fainted. A doctor was called, who at the station master's request joined the train for the rest of its bleak journey. At various points along the line the train stopped if it was close to where a victim's house lay, and at several places crowds had gathered to receive the remains of relatives. At Rosturk the train stopped again while Fathers Connolly and Fitzgerald of Achill, who had travelled from Westport, were called upon to console relatives. As the train continued, word had spread throughout the area that it was on its way, and such huge crowds turned out to pay their respects that over 40 Royal Irish Constabulary (RIC) men were needed to keep them off the railway line. It is not clear exactly where the partially built line beyond Mallaranny ended, but the train seems to have been able to get as far as the outskirts of the proposed Achill station, where black flags were put beside the track to mark the point where it was to stop. The train had left Newport at 12 noon, but did not reach here until after 2.00 pm. A long funeral procession took the dead across the (fairly new) road bridge onto the island, and down the coast road to Kildownet Cemetery, where they were all buried together in a large plot within the cemetery. The names of the dead included most of the well known families in the area - Malley, McLoughlin, Lavelle, Cafferkey, Mulloy, and Patten among them. The captain of the hooker, John Healy, survived but was reported to be badly affected by the incident: when the public inquiry took place only Patrick Sweeney (the other part-owner) attended. No blame was attached to the boat owners.

Many people in the area recollected a grim prophecy which local folklore had maintained for many years. In the 17th century, a local man named Brian Rua O'Cearbhain had predicted that one day 'carriages on iron wheels, emitting smoke and fire' would come to Achill. Their arrival, and their departure, would be marked with death. Little did they know how accurate this prophecy was to become, as two weeks before the line eventually closed in 1937, another train carried coffins.

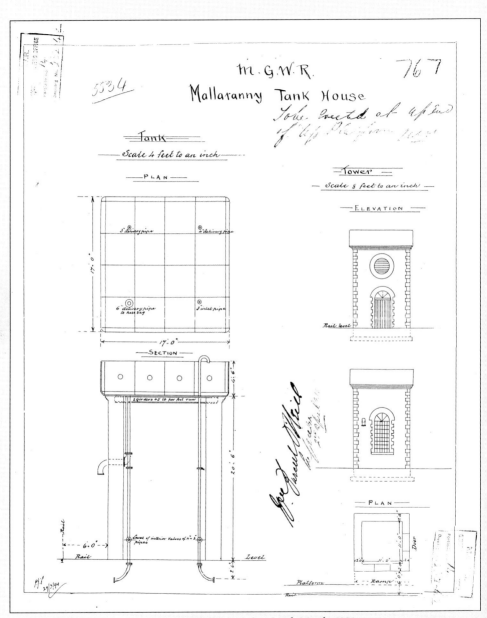

Engineer's drawing of Mallaranny water tower, dated 29th March, 1894.

H.C.A. Beaumont Collection

Section of trackbed near Owengarve River, 2000. The drainage channels on either side of the trackbed are still visible, choked with reeds.
Catherine Beaumont

Opening to Mallaranny

Major General Hutchinson undertook final inspection of the line from Newport to Mallaranny on 28th June. Worthington, O'Neill, and three others accompanied Hutchinson. It was agreed that the line could be opened on 11th July, providing the paperwork relating to authorised deviations from the original plans was completed, and the abutments of a bridge (probably the one over the Carrowsallagh River) were to be 'watched'.

In June 1894, the amended timetable for the line from Westport to Mallaranny was approved, and the line finally opened to traffic on 16th July, again without major fanfare. Since the station at Mallaranny was still not complete, a temporary wooden platform was in use, approximately where the goods platform eventually stood. Four days later, the Countess of Aberdeen visited the area, and she was conveyed by train on her return journey.

In the meantime, Barrington continued to press for further payment for work he had done. The company eventually offered Barrington £30 10s. in full settlement. Barrington claimed that the company's Engineer, Purcell O'Neill, had agreed that he was due some £550 or more.

O'Neill denied this, and the company reiterated their offer of £30 10s. Barrington returned the company's cheque for this amount, and demanded arbitration. The company told him to supply full details of what exactly he was claiming the £550 related to, but he did not do this. The correspondence dragged on for several months, before Barrington agreed to accept £114, the company having refused to go to arbitration throughout.

Now it was Worthington's turn! He requested a further payment of £307 for work in Newport station, but this was agreed without argument. And finally, a Patrick O'Dowd of Westport served a writ on the company for trespass and damage to his property during building work. It seems his claim was unsuccessful, as no payment was made to him and the matter was dropped.

Now, with trains running through to Mallaranny, the only outstanding items were completion of the permanent station there, and agreement with the Post Office about carriage of mails. The company informed the Post Office that the rate per mile would be based on that in operation elsewhere on the MGWR system, and that the 6.00 am goods train could carry mail.

RAILWAY STATION MOLRAHNY 6679 W.L.

Mallaranny station, soon after the line opened. An 'E' class 0-6-0 tank locomotive prepares to leave for Westport with a short goods train. Already, some subsidence is evident in the opposite platform, and a pile of bricks has been left by the builder to the right of the platform fence. It will be noted that no footbridge was provided at this station: passengers on the left-hand platform were required to cross the tracks by the footway connecting the platform ends throughout the life of the line.

Lawrence Collection, courtesy National Library of Ireland

Chapter Three

The Achill Extension Railway: Mallaranny to Achill

As already mentioned, the decision in principle to extend the Mallaranny railway to Achill Sound appears to have been taken following Balfour's visit to Achill in October 1890. The promoter of this section was the Board of Works, as opposed to the MGWR, so it was treated as a separate project throughout the period of construction. Certainly, the MGWR took care to distance itself from any of the planning involved, as will be seen. The contractor engaged to do the work was the same Robert Worthington who was involved with the Westport-Mallaranny line. The Achill Extension Railway Company (AER) was therefore formed, obtaining approval in July 1891 from the Grand Jury of County Mayo to commence operations. Following a survey the total cost of building this stretch of the line was estimated at £66,000 including materials. One intermediate station was proposed at Tonregee, about three miles east of the Achill terminus. Plans were drawn up for a two-storey station house and platform, but although no station was ever actually built there, trains stopped on request for a period to pick up or set down mails and passenger. In addition, a siding was laid beside the line to allow wagons to be loaded with fish from a nearby pier. This siding was little used, and is believed to have been disused by the mid-1910s.

Reference has already been made to the large numbers of local people employed in construction. For the Achill Extension, temporary housing was provided for the workmen just to the east of Achill station site, where they were accommodated in several large wooden dormitories. Contemporary reports suggest that the living conditions in these were of a very rudimentary nature!

In August, the BoW discussed with the MGWR what arrangements would be required at the Achill terminus for the servicing of locomotives. Much correspondence was to follow about the manner in which the MGWR might operate the railway, and the terms and conditions to be met before a working arrangement could be drawn up. But the railway company was unwilling to enter into any commitment until the whole line was complete and ready to operate. In July 1892 Mr J.G. Barton of the BoW wrote to the Chairman of the MGWR asking if the company would take it over and maintain it. They offered the MGWR a payment of £54,000 to do this. The MGWR replied that it would not consider this in any circumstances other than if and when the extension was totally completed to their standards.

The MGWR Engineer involved in negotiations was again Purcell O'Neill, who was also dealing with the Westport-Mallaranny contract. O'Neill perused the Achill Extension Company's proposals and reported that they required some improvement. He was unhappy with some of the alignments for the track bed, and with the proposals for installing water supplies at Achill itself. The proposed site of Achill station was an unstable turf bog, and much of the route of the Mallaranny - Achill section would have to cross ground of this nature. In August, further plans were submitted to the MGWR by the BoW, including

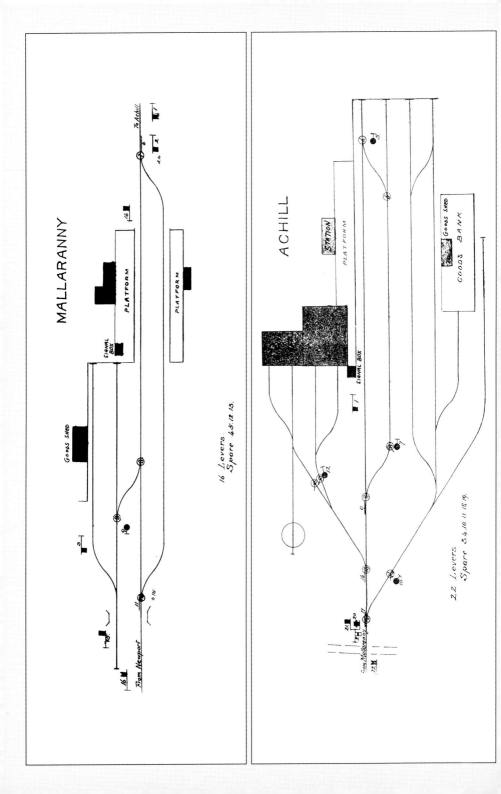

those for Achill station yard. They asked that O'Neill should meet with Barrington to discuss the plans. The company refused, saying that the line was not complete, and therefore no working agreement had been made, and it was nothing to do with them. At this stage the MGWR's Directors were occupied with the Mallaranny (and other) contracts, and had no inclination to be involved with the Achill Extension other than to clarify the AER's proposals at Mallaranny, so that the station there could be finished by Worthington. The BoW complained that the MGWR's conditions for operating the AER were 'impossible', but its protest fell on deaf ears. Numerous further requests were made about working agreements for the Achill section, but the company's refusals remained as adamant as the BoW's requests were numerous. In November 1892 the BoW told the MGWR that they 'wanted to accommodate' the company, and were 'prepared to meet to discuss the manner in which the line is to be completed'. It may be added that they had little choice but to accommodate the company fully, and to the company's specification, not theirs!

Finally, however, the Chairman and three other Directors of the MGWR met a deputation from the Board of Works. The company stipulated that before they would even consider working the line, the following extra conditions must be met:

- The BoW was not to assume that if any funds were saved in making Mallaranny station into a through station rather than a terminus, they would be re-directed towards equipping Achill as a terminus.
- Details for finishing the station at Mallaranny were to be finalised.
- Land was to be provided at Achill adjacent to the station for the construction of a hotel by the MGWR.
- The BoW was to arrange Government guarantees against losses incurred in working the Achill Extension.
- A partly-built pier behind Achill station was to be acquired and completed to a standard suitable for steamers to land at.

Following this meeting, the BoW wrote to the company recalling an agreement which they claimed had been made between Sir Ralph Cusack, MGWR Chairman, and Mr Jackson, Chief Secretary for Ireland, regarding the takeover of the AER by the MGWR. Sir Ralph disagreed, and the Company Secretary, G.W. Greene, replied to the BoW stating that Sir Ralph had made it quite clear to Mr Jackson both at the time and since, that under no circumstances would the MGWR take over the AER until and unless it was fully completed. The BoW persisted, repeating its request for the MGWR to become involved, and sending further plans of Achill station to the company's Engineer. It followed this with yet more requests for clarification on what the MGWR's terms were for operating the line. The company told the BoW that it was premature to send plans of Achill station. It seems that there were some in the Board of Works who were not only very persistent, but unwilling to accept what the railway company told them, as the MGWR had made its position absolutely clear from the outset, and had never wavered from it. However, the company responded by repeating its conditions as before, summarised in a letter to the BoW in which it was stated 'neither the Board of Directors nor their

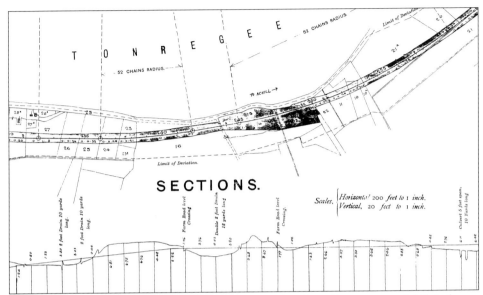

Engineer's drawing showing land allocated for proposed station at Tonregee, near Achill. In the end a siding was installed to allow loading of fish wagons, but it was little used and removed after some years. *H.C.A. Beaumont Collection*

The site of Tonregee fish siding. The line from Mallaranny approached past the small house roof in the middle left of the picture, and ran through where the barn now stands, and to the right of the bushes on the right hand side. The siding diverged at the far end of the barn, and continued towards the foreground. *Author*

Chairman ever agreed to take over and work the AER until it has been completed to the satisfaction of the company's Chief Engineer'. However the company did also repeat that it would be interested in operating the line once all its conditions were met.

Work was in progress, however, and by June 1893 Sir Ralph was able to inspect the completed work the whole way to Achill. O'Neill was instructed to draw up an outline working agreement to present to the MGWR Board. Plans included the construction of a railway-owned hotel at Achill, and two possible sites were considered. One location was opposite the station; it is not known where the other was. A water supply for the new Achill station was arranged - this was taken from the nearby Loughan Lake.

In May 1893 the Board of Works agreed to pay £2,800 in instalments to the MGWR towards maintenance and drainage of turf bogs adjacent to the route of the new line. In addition, a draft agreement was signed between the BoW and the company on 7th February, 1894, in which the following points were made:

- The MGWR was to operate at least two trains per day between Achill and Mallaranny in each direction to carry passengers. If mixed trains were not allowed by the Board of Trade, a separate goods train was to run as well.
- The Treasury was to pay the MGWR £3,000 in lieu of future maintenance on handing over the line.
- Buildings, water columns and the locomotive turntable at Achill were to be to the MGWR's pattern or specification, while all signals were to be to Railway Signal Co. pattern. The goods crane at Achill was to have a capacity of 1½ tons, and a weighing machine of ½ ton capacity was to be installed.
- Finally, a station and buildings at Claggan Ferry (between Tonregee and Mallaranny) were to be built to MGWR plans.

It should be added that no station at Claggan Ferry was ever built. The Claggan station related to a one time proposal to build a line from this point on the Achill line to Belmullet, via a long viaduct across Bellacragher Bay to the north of Mayo. This, along with other equally abortive schemes to build a railway to Belmullet, is dealt with in the next chapter.

By March 1894 the work was largely complete and preparations were made to open the line. In April, the official inspection by Major Addison from the BoW took place. Addison was generally satisfied, despite the fact that when he attempted to alight from the train at Mallaranny, the door of the carriage struck a protruding rock beside the line when opened! This 'knob of rock' was removed with appropriate haste. Addison's only observation was that the flooring in the waiting shelter on the down platform was to be completed. He added that staff were to be warned about the severity of the gradient on the mile of line just west of Mallaranny station, where the line dropped down to almost sea level at 1 in 70.

In May 1894 another inspection confirmed that a number of matters still required completion. In consequence, the first train ran to Achill on 13th May 1895, some 18 months later than originally anticipated. The first train was hauled by one of the new 'E' class locomotives, No. 110 *Bat*. The driver was J. Byrne, and the fireman was named McLean, and the train was received by the newly appointed station master, Mr Tully. Achill, at last, had entered the Railway Age.

Achill station, 1895 - just after the line was opened. On the left is Holy Trinity Church of Ireland (now closed) and in the foreground the temporary workmen's living accommodation may be seen. Over 20 years later, some of these buildings were still extant, one at least being rented out as a dwelling! In the station itself, two wagons loaded with planks may be seen, as well as a line of goods vans beside the goods shed. A long line of open wagons, believed to belong to the contractor who built the line, remain parked in the long seaward siding. The extensive nature of the station layout is evident: events were to prove this to be over-optimistic after only a few years. *Lawrence Collection, courtesy National Library of Ireland*

The end of the line at Achill 1895. A lone wagon sits at the end of the goods siding. The wagon is a standard convertible van (or 'soft-top') - a type of wagon used by many Irish railways to carry general goods (with canvas cover over the centre of the roof), or cattle (with the cover removed to allow air to circulate). The railway has just opened for business, and Alexander Hector's fish store has yet to be built beside the line. Achill Island lies just across the water. *Lawrence Collection, courtesy National Library of Ireland*

Chapter Four

Proposals for Other Railways

At the time the Achill line was promoted, high hopes abounded for a network of other railways in the area. These were variously intended to develop poor areas or to allow access to harbour facilities that had been proposed in several locations. Other than the Achill line, the short Westport Quay line, and the Ballina-Killala line, none of these was ever built.

Belmullet

In February 1890, the first reference to plans for a railway to Belmullet involved a proposal submitted to the Lord Lieutenant for Ireland by a consortium of clergy and businessmen from the area. Belmullet, and the area around it, was at the time very remote indeed, and the road system was inadequate for anything other than horse-drawn carts. The MGWR decided to express 'dissent', fearing that pressure would be put on the company to become involved in a project of this nature. The company, unsurprisingly, took the view that any other line in this district would be unlikely to contribute any financial benefit, running as it would through one of the remotest areas in Ireland. It was decided that a company engineer and a locally recruited solicitor were to attend such meetings to defend the company's interests.

In September 1890, a public meeting was called in Belmullet by a Mr James May, who appears to have been a local businessman. A resolution was passed in favour of contacting the MGWR Board to ask if they would meet a deputation of 11 people who would present a case for extending the Ballina-Killala line to Belmullet, via Ballycastle. The railway company agreed to meet five people, and adopted a cautious stance. No sooner had this happened, than Revd P. O'Reilly of the same area presented the company with another proposal, which would involve building a line from Westport to Belmullet, via Newport, Mallaranny, Ballycroy and Bangor Erris. The company simply acknowledged his letter and left it at that.

By now, considerable public interest had been aroused, and Revd O'Reilly again pressed the company to agree to work a line to Belmullet. The MGWR replied that it was not prepared to consider any extension lines in the West of Ireland at this stage.

A new plan was prepared, for a proposed Killala, Ballycastle and Belmullet Light Railway. The MGWR was again asked to work it, and again it refused, but qualified this by saying that it would give consideration to a line as far as Ballycastle only.

In 1893, the plans for the Achill Extension Railway from Mallaranny to Achill were in progress. A proposal was made that a line to Belmullet would branch off this line at a point close to Owenduff, some four miles beyond Mallaranny. The new line would continue due north to a point at which it could cross the inlet of Bellacragher Bay by a long viaduct of several spans, and continue north

Proposed Railways in West Mayo/Achill Area 1890-1910

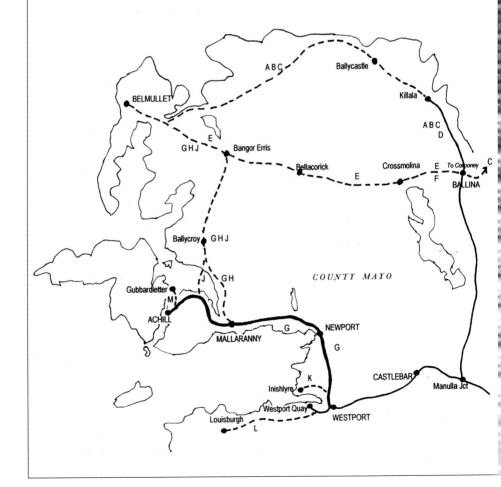

▬▬▬ Achill line as built   --------------- Other railways

-------- Line planned but never built

A Belmullet - Ballina via Ballycastle proosed by J May, 1890 and Dougherty, 1906
B Killala, Ballycastle & Belmullet Railway
C Collooney, Ballina & Belmullet Railway, proposed 1907
D Ballycastle - Killala railway, proposed 1891 & 1895
E Belmullet - Crossmolina - Ballina railway, proposed by O'Reilly & Crilly, 1895, and Rev. R. Conmy, 1897
F Ballina - Crossmolina railway, proposed by Fraser, 1891 and 1895
G Westport - Mallaranny - Bangor - Belmullet railway, proposed by Rev. O'Reilly 1890
H Mallaranny - Belmullet railway, proposed by local businessmen, 1895, by Verkehr 1897, and by Worthington 1910
J Mallaranny - Belmullet railway, proposed by W G Murphy 1893 & 1896, J T Power 1899, and Flynn 1906
K Inishlyre extension, proposed 1894 - 1903
L Westport - Louisburgh railway, proposed 1895
M Gubbardletter extension, Achill; proposed 1897

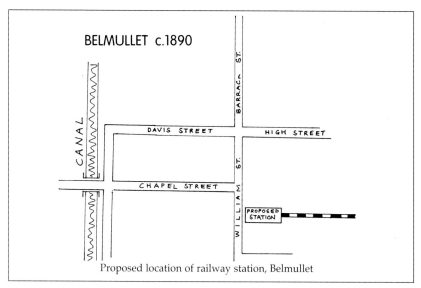

Proposed location of railway station, Belmullet

towards Ballycroy. Such a line would have been very expensive to build, and would have traversed some 30 miles of almost totally uninhabited and unproductive land, before ending at Belmullet. Surprisingly, the company agreed to carry out an inspection of the proposed route, following which it decided to hold discussions with the Government about whether the line should continue from this point for some four miles to Achill Sound, or for some 30 northwards to Belmullet. However, the company's Directors still felt that they were being pressurised into becoming involved with a project they saw no benefit in, and they insisted that any discussions they held be 'without prejudice'. Within two months, plans forged ahead for the Achill option, and the Belmullet scheme was dropped.

A Mr O'Donel wrote to the company at this stage claiming that the Canadian Government was prepared to give a grant or subsidy towards the establishment of a transatlantic port in the area. He suggested that the company extend the line from Mallaranny for a distance of 16 miles in the direction of Belmullet, to a point where this could be built. The company replied that it would require details of what was on offer. No further correspondence took place!

In 1895, the Revd O'Reilly came to the company's attention once again. He had circulated a pamphlet in the Belmullet area extolling the virtues of Blacksod Bay as a location for a transatlantic port for Canadian mail ships. He asked the railway company to pay for the printing and distribution of his pamphlet - hardly surprisingly they refused, but (doubtless tongue-in-cheek!) told O'Reilly that once he had published it, they would buy a few copies! The Clerk of Belmullet Union, perhaps stirred by the pamphlet, urged the Government to subsidise the construction of a railway to serve the proposed port as well as Belmullet. The company, seeing a possible distraction from demands that they waste shareholders' money, now offered to subsidise Revd O'Reilly's pamphlet. Petitions now appeared from a group in Ballina asking for the company to become involved in a Ballina-Belmullet railway, while another group which included representatives from Westport Union sent a deputation to the Government asking for a railway to be built from 'Mallaranny or Claggan Ferry' to Belmullet. A public meeting was called, at which the proposals were endorsed. The company made no comment, waiting instead to see if any further plans were put forward. It appears that the Government made no commitment to do anything, so the scheme foundered yet again. Some months later, two more groups met company representatives. The first was led by a Mr Crilly, the local Member of Parliament, and two Parish Priests from the area. They pressed the case for the Ballina-Belmullet route again. The second deputation, led by Revd P.J. Nolan, suggested the Ballina-Killala-Ballycastle-Belmullet route. Both these groups agreed on one point only: that the western route from Mallaranny would be of no benefit to North Mayo, whereas either of their schemes would. The company could hardly disagree with this, but held out against involvement. However, they re-iterated their interest in a line to Ballycastle, and perhaps to be tactful, said that they would give consideration to working a line to Crossmolina, despite having objected to this four years earlier.

Belmullet Board of Guardians of Belmullet Union now joined the clamour, doubtless prepared to welcome a railway from any of the three proposed routes - again, the company remained silent.

However, by May 1896 the transatlantic port proposal was now being taken seriously by the company. The Chairman, Major Cusack, and Captain Smyth joined a group to meet representatives of the Canadian Government in London. The company arranged for three local promoters from Belmullet, including E.T. O'Donel, to travel with them free of charge. One of the original promoters of a line from the Mallaranny direction, W.G. Murphy, reminded them that the new Act promoting the building of tramways and light railways might be of benefit, in that a line via Claggan Ferry would now be a more viable proposition. The company stated that they would take no action until they saw what plans the Government had first. Yet again, no further progress was made with any of the schemes.

By 1897, another group of businessmen in Ballina had called in more senior clergy to support their entreaties to the company, in the shape of the Bishop, the Most Revd Dr Conmy. The company gave the now standard response and thanked them for their interest in a railway from there to Belmullet, and expressed regret that it would not become involved in the proposal. The company was now becoming frustrated with the seemingly endless petitions, deputations, and meetings being called to promote the various schemes. A German businessman, Herr Verkehr, who again raised the issue of the route via Ballycroy, was curtly told that the company could do nothing.

Two years later, the clamour had not died down. A Mr James Talbot Power produced a new plan for a railway to Belmullet via Claggan Ferry, and presumably running from Mallaranny. The company, in exasperation, wrote to him and told him that it had 'already told the promoters of four other lines that the company will do nothing until the Government's intentions are known regarding the route and the source of funding'. Power, undeterred, petitioned the Chief Secretary for Ireland, who told him there was 'no use in meeting'. Power wrote to the railway company again, and received a reply from Major Cusack reiterating what he had said before. However, Cusack added that he would favour this route, as it was 'little more than half the distance of the other four routes proposed'. This, though, was subject to the Government building and equipping the line, and generally providing all the guarantees necessary to ensure that if the MGWR worked the line, they would not have to bear any operating loss it incurred. It was also to be built to the same specification as the Clifden and Achill lines.

The company's stance was clear, and no further developments took place for some years. However, in 1906 a Mr Flynn of Belmullet, whose wife ran a hotel there, proposed a line from Claggan to Belmullet, presumably connected to the Achill line near Mallaranny or Owenduff. The can of worms was open again: the Killala to Belmullet rival scheme now resurfaced, championed by Sir J.B. Dougherty, who asked the company whether they would prefer to link Belmullet to the railway system via Mr Flynn's route, or his. Mr J. Rutledge, of the Westport Harbour Commissioners, added his voice to the clamour and asked for a meeting with the company, who refused this request.

The Government, finally, began to carry out some preparatory work. An engineer was dispatched to draw up plans of a line from Killala to Belmullet, and in 1907 Rutledge promoted a Bill in Parliament called 'Colloney, Ballina and Belmullet Railways and Piers Bill'. A petition of 54 company shareholders who lived in the area was submitted to the Company Secretary in support of the scheme. Three further petitions in favour of the scheme had been received from the Bellacorick, Belmullet and Bangor areas. The MGWR's Directors admitted that nothing in the plans would be likely to put the company's position in jeopardy, and they agreed to meet with Government representatives in Dublin. The Government offered to pay the company £4,000 per mile to build the line, and work it in perpetuity. Before the company had time to consider this, the offer was amended to a one-off grant of £135,000 to build the line to Belmullet from whatever direction the MGWR saw fit.

Needless to say, nothing came of this, and by now both sides were exasperated. Dougherty wrote to the company to say that he now felt 'released from any engagement with the company', and added that he would now consider that he could negotiate with any other party to build or operate the line. This can only have been good news to the company. It may be noted that neither Dougherty, nor anybody else, had ever had any 'engagement' with the company over a railway to Belmullet!

In 1910, Worthington, the contractor involved in the building of both the Achill line and other railways operated by the MGWR, informed the company that he had the means to raise the £135,000 mentioned earlier. He asked the company if it would operate a Mallaranny-Belmullet line if he would build it. The Company Secretary told him that given the long history of proposals in the area, they would not now support any route to Belmullet. This concluded the matter, though hardly to the satisfaction of many, and no further plans were made to bring rails to Belmullet.

A plan has survived showing the proposed location of the station in Belmullet - this is believed to be part of the plan undertaken by the Government's Engineer in 1907. It is noted that the proposed terminus would have been 25½ miles from Mallaranny. A tunnel at Dooghill, near Ballycroy, would have been included in this scheme. A school atlas published about 1910 actually showed a line from Ballina to Belmullet.

Crossmolina

In 1891 a scheme promoted by a Mr Fraser went as far as planning stage, the MGWR Board being shown detailed plans of a proposed junction at Ballina, from where a line would be built to Crossmolina. The steepest gradient would have been 1 in 80, and the proposal was that the MGWR would work the line. The company's Engineer reported that the plan for the junction was 'objectionable', and the promoter was duly informed. The company informed the Clerk of Ballina Union (the local authority) that it would not be in their shareholder's interests to be involved with this scheme, and consequently they refused to discuss it further.

However, the promoters persisted. They put forward another scheme which would involve the Killala line being extended to Ballycastle, and said they would purchase one locomotive. The company replied that they ruled out the Crossmolina line, but said that the Ballycastle line would be 'a possibility', provided they received 100 per cent of the receipts!

After this, Crossmolina featured in various plans as one of the intermediate places on a line from Ballina to Belmullet, but no further proposals were made suggesting it as a terminus in itself.

Inishlyre

In 1894, the MGWR Board received a letter from the Congested Districts Board (CDB) offering to pay for a jetty at 'Inishlyre Roads', on the coast a few miles outside Westport. They maintained that they understood that the company was planning to build a deep water port there. The company was taken by surprise, and replied immediately that not only had it never planned to build any port in the area, but it had no funds to do so either. Nothing further came of the scheme until 1901, when the CDB and the Department of Agriculture asked if the company would build a siding to this proposed port. To describe this as a 'siding' was something of an over-simplification, as the line would have been several miles in length, branching off the Achill line just outside Westport. The cost was to be £20,000, and the company was asked to provide half this cost and the CDB a quarter. Needless to say, the company declined to become involved. The CDB then offered to pay half of the overall cost, but the MGWR replied in the same way as it had done when faced with similar requests for other schemes: if the line was built to the company's standards, by somebody else, the company would work the line. This must have encouraged the CDB, as they now asked the company to build a station at Inishlyre.

The familiar sequence of persuasive letters, petitions and meetings now followed. Representatives of the shipping line, Cunard, met with the Board of Works and the MGWR's General Manager (Cusack) to ascertain what involvement the railway company could have in a railway connection, station and port at Inishlyre. This time the company agreed to become involved, and Cusack offered to pay a third of the overall cost. The Board of Works subsequently wrote to Cusack expressing disappointment at that amount, whereupon Cusack replied that his Board of Directors would not increase this offer. He went on to say that the company could not become involved in the operation of steamers from Inishlyre to Tonregee - this presumably being another scheme that had been mentioned at the meeting.

The BoW asked the company to clarify exactly what their requirements would be for the operation of such a line. Some years earlier, an equivalent and lengthy correspondence had taken place between the two regarding the building, funding and operation of the Achill Extension Railway. The company repeatedly made its position crystal clear, only to be asked to reconsider time and time again. The impression can be had that the company was endlessly patient in dealing with all this correspondence!

Nonetheless, the company's Manager, Tatlow, and Engineer, O'Neill, were dispatched to meet the BoW, who asked them to reconsider their terms as stated. The company now replied that it would be prepared to extend the Westport Quay line to a new port in deeper water, but they would not build the line that the BoW wanted, off the Westport-Newport line. The BoW said they would be forced to abandon the scheme if the company insisted on this. This news constituted a relief to the company, rather than a threat, and they did not waver from what they had already stated.

But the BoW was not satisfied, and as a result of their appeals, the Lord Lieutenant for Ireland now wrote to the MGWR offering to pay for the pier, if the company would subscribe £15,000 towards the cost of the connecting line. This time the company had had enough, and the Secretary wrote back in distinctly frosty tones, making the following points:

1. The company would have nothing to do with the scheme, or any of its plans, until it saw definite proposals. It made the point that these plans had already been promised, but had not materialised.
2. It told the BoW that rates for carrying traffic over the line would be the same as anywhere else - no discounts or special consideration would be given.
3. It asked whether the BoW intended to maintain the pier and associated works.

The plans arrived with the company two months later. Westport Urban Council enquired about progress, and the company told them that the whole scheme was 'in the Government's hands'. Another frosty letter was sent by the MGWR's Secretary to the Government complaining about the extent of the role that the company was expected to play in the Inishlyre project, and the cost involved. He attacked the proposals themselves, saying that the company would not move from its stated position at all, and would have no involvement at all unless the Government built the line and all associated works, and paid for it in full, and agreed to maintain it for ever. When the BoW wrote back saying that they had never intended that the company maintain it, the MGWR's attitude softened. It replied to the BoW to say that once the line was built, they would maintain the railway line itself, but not the harbour.

Perhaps this was a mistake, as the begging letters started again. The BoW wanted a meeting, but the company told them clear plans were to be drawn up first. The BoW replied that they would send the plans in after the meeting - whereupon the company simply told them that in that case, there was no point in having a meeting.

The BoW, not to be outdone, produced plans for through fares for passengers from various ports in Great Britain, via Dublin, Westport and Inishlyre, via boat from there to Tonregee, and on to Belmullet! Finally, plans were provided of the engineering works proposed. The MGWR noted that the plans were very detailed when it came to the harbour facilities, but sketchy on the railway connection. Where railway details were proposed, the company pointed out that a proposed track alignment had an impossibly tight curve, and no guard rails were provided on the pier siding. In addition, the pier had no water supply for either steam boats or locomotives. The BoW said they did not see any necessity to plan the railway exactly until the pier was partly built - in spite of the company's repeated insistence on seeing the plans for the 'siding'.

Almost unbelievably, the Rt Hon. Sir A.P. McDonnell, Under Secretary for Ireland, wrote to the company in 1905 saying that if it failed to carry out what he saw as its obligation to be involved in the way that the BoW wanted, the surrounding areas would be greatly disadvantaged as a result and the 'intention of the Government would be frustrated'. A speedy reply from the long-suffering Company Secretary referred him to previous correspondence, and made it clear that the company had no wish to stand in the way of any proposed scheme. However, he pointed out, the Congested Districts Board had initiated all of this, and the MGWR held no liability in any respect whatever. The Under Secretary replied, saying that he thought that the MGWR had intended to operate a steamer from Tonregee to Belmullet themselves! This was not the case, and never had been. The company did not reply to him; the MGWR Secretary wearily complained to Westport councillors that 'this correspondence with three departments (CDB, BoW, and Government) had been going on for five years . . .'

The Under Secretary wrote, asking for a reply to his earlier letter - this time he got one, dated 16th May, 1905. It outlined the company's position.

1. The MGWR had considered Inishlyre and Tonregee-Belmullet as one issue all along.
2. The landing of fish at Tonregee had now ceased (and with it the use of the fish siding there) [see Chapter Seven].
3. It was the CDB who had persuaded the company to install the fish siding in the first place, and it had proved to be of no benefit to the company. (Presumably it was of little benefit to the local people as well, judging by the very low usage of it while it was in operation.)
4. The Government had made no effort to start the Tonregee-Belmullet part of the scheme.
5. Without the Government paying for the entire construction costs, the benefit to the company would be nil.

The letter ended by saying that due to the long delay, the fall in the company's shares in recent years, and the difficulties the company faced in other areas, the company's Directors and shareholders would not sanction any funding for any such projects. This had the desired effect, and no further plans were made.

Gubbardletter

In May 1897, the Board of Works submitted plans to the company for a line from Achill station to Gubbardletter. This is a remote location some two miles from Achill station. The line would have branched off the existing line about one mile from Achill, and continued north for approximately one further mile, to end at a pier. The BoW wanted a pier built there to assist local fisherman, and to receive steamers, with trains connecting it to Achill station. Gubbardletter Point did not have any road access, nor indeed any form of development at all, and the whole scheme would have been constructed on what is known nowadays as a 'green field site'. The railway company objected on grounds of cost and safety, arguing that with no road access, people would inevitably use the railway line as a footpath, and this would result in a risk of being hit by a train. The BoW accepted this point, but persisted. A draft agreement was drawn up, in which the company stipulated the following conditions:

1. The track was to be the same as the rest of the Achill line.
2. The company would provide a wagon turntable, but not a locomotive turntable, at the pier.
3. The station building at Gubbardletter was not to cost the company more than £100.
4. The line was to be worked under control of the main line staff between Mallaranny and Achill.
5. The junction with the Achill line was to be controlled by a signal box.
6. Locomotives were to run to and from, and be serviced at, Achill; not the junction.
7. The trains would run in connection with steamer services.
8. A road was to be planned to avoid pedestrians or cattle walking along the railway.
9. The Board of Works had been proposing steamer services in the area that would have competed with trains between Achill and Westport. These were not to run, or the company would pull out of any agreement to operate the line to Gubbardletter.

At this stage, common sense prevailed. A line such as this would have been of absolutely minimal benefit to anybody, and nothing further came of it.

Other Proposals

Another new line was proposed in October 1895. This line would have left Westport, possible as an extension of the Quay line, and would have run out along the south side of Clew Bay as far as Louisburgh. It was proposed to the MGWR in a letter from the Westport Union, the local authority of the day. The MGWR simply ignored the suggestions, and nothing further came of the scheme. The proposed line would have been about nine miles long, and would have passed through no place of significant population *en route*.

In the first few years of the 20th century, several vague proposals were made for an extension of the Achill line onto Achill Island. Had this line been built, it would been a very scenic stretch of railway, crossing Achill Sound on a bridge before continuing through wild and beautiful scenery to the north of the island, arriving at the picturesque seaside village of Dugort. In 1907, a Revd Colleran wrote to the company asking about a 'proposed railway' to Keel, in the west of Achill Island. Needless to say, the company had no proposals of the sort in mind.

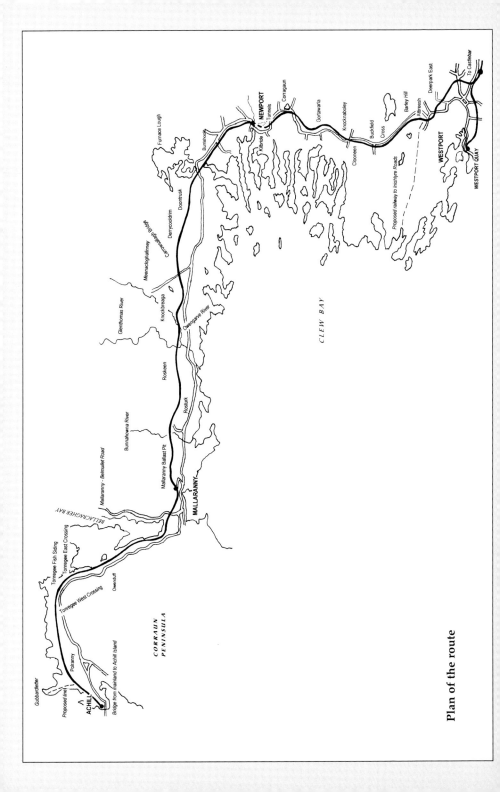

Plan of the route

Chapter Five

A Journey over the Line

Several graphic descriptions of travel over the railway have survived, and give a good idea not only of what it was like to undertake a railway journey to Achill, but also what the general conditions in the area were like. The following article was published in a tourist brochure in 1902.

At the west end of the Westport town station the metals of the Achill line curve sharply to the right and cross the valley by a fine stone viaduct. We see little of Westport itself, a small seaport of some 4,000 inhabitants and the centre of the shipping trade of the district. The town has lately become noted as the birthplace of the Irish Land League. It lies at the head of Clew Bay, and the approach to the harbour passes between the hundreds of green islets, emeralds of the sea, that stud the upper end of that mountain-sheltered nook of the Atlantic.

The railway hence to Achill was built by the help of the Government with money granted by the Light Railways (Ireland) Act of 1889, during Mr A.J. Balfour's Chief Secretaryship, and is therefore what is known as a 'Balfour Light Railway'. It is, however, light more in name than anything else, for the permanent way, station buildings and signalling are all of a substantial order. To a great extent however the line follows the contour of the ground, so that gradients are heavy, and the only large works are two stone viaducts and two short tunnels, all in the first eight miles.

After we have crossed the Westport viaduct we leave the woods, and the line winds its way among treeless green *kopjes* (no other word describes these hillocks so aptly) curving right and left alternately like a watercourse in its efforts to find the lowest level. Though but a short distance away on our left the sea is not yet visible. At length we pass through the two short tunnels before-mentioned, and then cross the river, which is called after the town of Newport, by another stone viaduct of seven arches, with picturesque up and down stream views. At the end of the bridge is Newport station, 7¾ miles from Westport.

The Irish light railways of standard gauge differ much from the narrow-gauge lines, such as the Donegal, West Clare, and Tralee and Dingle, in this point of the spacing of stations. On the 26 miles from Westport to Achill there are but two intermediate stations, while on the 31 miles from Tralee to Dingle the trains will call at 15 stations. That line runs mostly beside the road, and many of the 'stations' are but stopping places with little more than a nameboard. There is not much to choose between the two districts as regards population, and the scarcity of stations must surely lessen the usefulness of such railways. No cottage on the Tralee and Dingle line is more than a mile or two from a station, and all the country folk use the railway for weekly marketing purposes. Here in Mayo a man's potato-patch may adjoin the railway and yet be 5 miles from a station.

Newport station is a substantial red brick structure [*Author's note: it was in fact built from cut stone, like the viaduct; the writer of this article clearly confused it with the building at Mallaranny*] with two platforms and a passing loop. Soon after leaving it the line approaches the range of heather-clad mountains that rise from the northern shore of Clew Bay, then it bends westward and pursues an undulating course along their lower slopes.

We pass in sight of Lough Feeagh, a placid sheet of water stretching away northward into the bosom of the hills, then the green pasture land gives place to bog and heather, streaked with tumbling mountain torrents. The line runs at a height of several hundred feet above sea level in order to avoid the closely-cultivated land that fringes the shore. Bogland is cheaper for railway purposes than pasture or arable. At intervals between the many cuttings we see glimpses of Clew Bay and the great mass of Croagh Patrick rising

45

Achill Branch (Westport to Achill)

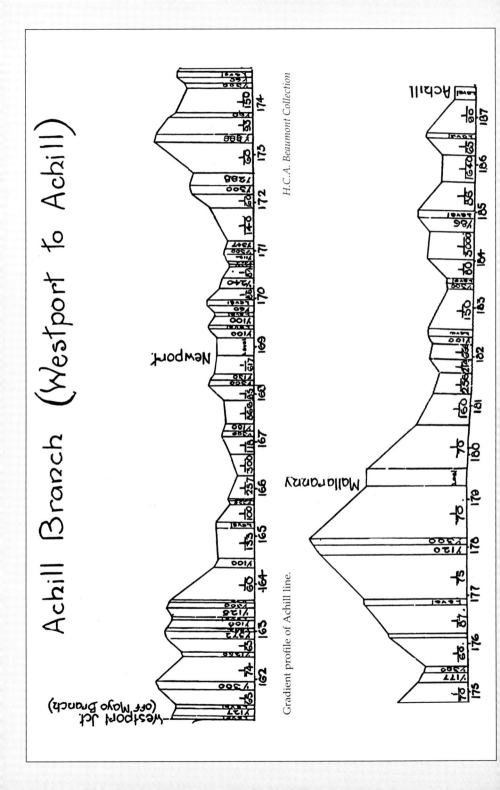

Gradient profile of Achill line.

H.C.A. Beaumont Collection

from its southern shore 10 miles across the blue water. Our train puffs slowly up a long bank mostly of 1 in 60, and 1 in 75, then it rounds a spur of the hills and Mallaranny comes in sight. A rush of a mile or so downhill brings us to the station, a replica of the one at Newport. (*See earlier note: the two station buildings were in fact quite different.*)

This is a small straggling village, whose name is spelt by the Post Office 'Mulrany', and the Ordnance Survey 'Molreny', and is pronounced 'M'lranny'. It is set in a sheltered nook of the hills, where the view of Croagh Patrick and Clew Bay is finest. Everywhere is a luxuriant growth of fuchsia, the road, railway, hedges and gardens are lined with dense hedges of it, and the masses of blue and red blossom amid the purple heather give a wonderful colouring to the landscape. Rhododendron, bog-myrtle, London pride, and numberless other plants run wild about this oasis of the mountains. Hard by the station the railway company have built a large hotel, modern and comfortable, whither summer and winter visitors come from far and near to enjoy the beauties of the spot itself, to fish the neighbouring rivers, play golf, and to use it as a base for the exploration of Achill Island.

There is one deficiency at Mallaranny, and that is the absence of churches, both Catholic and Protestant. Therefore on Sunday mornings a special train runs to Newport and back for the spiritual benefit of all and sundry, principally hotel visitors. It is not often that Sunday trains have the effect of filling the churches, but then Ireland is a land of contraries.

The hotel and station are set some 200 ft above the shore on the neck of an isthmus. Taking up our journey to Achill, we leave the station on a downward gradient of 1 in 70, and in a few seconds come in sight of a long inland sea winding away northward to meet the Atlantic at Blacksod Bay. Bellacragher Bay, as it is called, resembles a lake, and it is not until we notice the long fringe of seaweed lying between the water and the heather that we realise that this is the sea itself.

The 8 miles of line that end at Achill Sound pass through as desolate a region as any in the British Isles. To the left of the line wide stretches of heather-clad bog and mountain rise to meet the skyline at 2,000 ft or so, to the right is more bog, then the winding inland sea, then more heathery mountains. Houses are few and far between, and at the best are but wretched mud cabins, each with its patch of poor wind-beaten oats and its little bed of osiers. Women in red petticoats, and men in knee-breeches, stand at their doors to watch the train pass. This is Ireland indeed.

At length, we pass a distant signal, and a moment later pull up at Achill station, the terminus of the line, 26 miles from Westport. This is a well-built station, with a refreshment-room and a yard full of fish vans awaiting the harvest of the sea, which forms the bulk of the east-going traffic. The railway ends on the mainland close by Achill Sound; here is a narrow strip of salt water swirling under the iron swing bridge that carries the road across to Achill Island. A tiny hotel stands beside the station, and on either side of the Sound a scattered fishing village straggles along the dreary road. The scenery is wild and treeless, the same great stretches of heathery bog and mountain and winding inland sea, as the train has passed for miles.

The road goes winding over the hills to Dugort, the principal village of the island, and possibly the future terminus of the railway. Dugort is an angler's paradise known to a select few.

Thither over the intervening 8 miles of road visitors are conveyed on one of the 'long cars' belonging to the Midland Great Western Railway, which awaits our train at Achill station.

A tourist guide published by the MGWR in 1907 described the line as 'interesting and beautiful throughout. To avoid a monstrous tunnel through the mountain mass of the Corraun Peninsula the line makes a great sweep round its northern half. To begin with we get on the left, boldly scarped bluffs, and then on the right, strike Bellacragher Bay'. One wonders what Worthington and O'Neill would have made of a proposal to build such a tunnel!

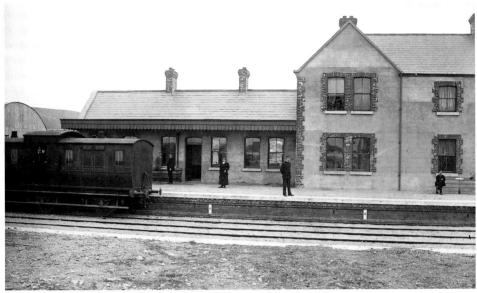

Achill station, just after the line opened. This view is taken from the goods platform, as yet not properly surfaced. The passenger brake coach is the then new No. 19, built in 1896. After the Achill line was closed, this vehicle survived in traffic elsewhere until 1956.

Lawrence Collection, courtesy National Library of Ireland

A very rare view of hardship relief supplies being unloaded at Achill, shortly after the line opened. The worst effects of the Great Famine in Ireland were evident from the mid-1840s to the late 1850s, but severe poverty afflicted the Achill area until the end of the 19th century. In this photograph, wagons of grain are being unloaded at the end of the goods yard, from a traditional Irish 'soft-top' convertible wagon. The 'Guinness' van has presumably been pressed into service to carry bags of grain! *Irish Railway Record Society*

Chapter Six

The Early Years

No sooner was the line open the whole way to Achill, than the MGWR's Mr Tatlow organised the first excursion trains. On 23rd June, 1895 two heavily loaded trains brought what was probably Achill Island's first-ever mass of day trippers for a seven hour stay. Cheap third class fares were offered, the trains both originating in Castlerea, Co. Roscommon, picking up passengers between there and Mallaranny. The visitors were welcomed with cheers by a crowd of islanders waiting at the road bridge, and the whole day's operations were considered a great success.

Some details of early train workings have survived. On 10th July, 1894 return journeys could be made at single fare from stations on the line to Westport for the race meeting there, and to Newport for the duration of the 'bathing season'. However, a request for an extra train from Achill to Westport Quay in September for a race meeting was declined, the company stating that existing services were adequate. Residents of the Ballycroy area (north of Mallaranny) complained that there was only the one through service to Dublin each day, and that the facilities on this were unsuitable for the carriage of fish; and the train reached Dublin too late for the fish markets anyway. Nothing was done at this stage in response, but an extra service was introduced soon afterwards. This was a mixed train, the return working of which left Westport at 1.30 pm, arriving in Achill at 3.15 pm. The slow timing of this train, taking 1¾ hours to travel 27 miles, was due to a long wait at Newport for the existing 1.35 departure from Achill to cross it.

In June 1896, return tickets at single fare were provided for the Achill Regatta. This was an important event in the neighbourhood, and the area around Achill Sound played host to races on the sand and a variety of sideshows and travelling salesmen. The MGWR agreed to pay 5 per cent of receipts from these tickets to the Regatta organisers. The same arrangement was made in subsequent years for a period. In Mallaranny, another regatta was held regularly which also resulted in special traffic arrangements.

A number of other imaginative efforts to attract traffic were made in the line's early years. In 1899, horses were conveyed free to Westport Races in addition to the normal offer of return at single fare for all passengers. Similar offers were applied to travel to Mallaranny for the Regatta there, and between Westport and Mallaranny or Achill each Thursday, the market day. By 1900, an annual Sports Day at Mallaranny was also attracting considerable traffic at discounted rates. Cheap fares to Achill were available from as far afield as Ballinrobe, Killala, and Castlerea.

Overall traffic levels showed healthy growth in the first few years of the line's life. In 1898 the MGWR ordered 30 extra cattle wagons to cope with traffic on some lines, including the Achill line. Tourist traffic continued to flourish as well, and much transhipment of passenger's trunks and suitcases had to be undertaken at Achill, with a variety of jaunting cars and horse-drawn carts meeting trains. In those days, nobody travelled light!

In March 1897 the MGWR Board 'learned with great surprise from the newspapers' that the Congested Districts Board intended to run a steamer

RAILWAY TERMINUS ACHILL 6794. W.L.

Achill station soon after opening. This photograph is of interest in showing builder's materials still scattered at the trackside. The locomotive seen shunting the passenger brake coach is one of the 'E' class tank engines supplied in 1891 for the opening of various branch lines. Originally No. 110 (named *Bat*), this locomotive survived as GSR/CIE No. 555 until 1955 (*see photograph on page 90*). Left of centre may be seen the roofed-over carriage shed, between the signal box and the locomotive shed. One coach is parked inside. A train has just arrived at the platform, consisting of the then standard set of three six-wheeled coaches and a van, with the usual array of wagons in tow. The locomotive has just run round the train, and has taken the van from the back in readiness to shunt the wagons.

Lawrence Collection, courtesy National Library of Ireland

service from Westport to Achill from April 1898. They protested strongly in a letter from G.W. Greene (the MGWR Company Secretary) to the CDB. They pointed out (at length) the work they had done in bringing the railway to Achill and the growing traffic levels on the railway. They asked the CDB to scrap their plans, and to confirm in writing that they had done this. But the CDB replied that what they had already said, they could not recede from. Some further correspondence was exchanged; the MGWR pointing out that the CDB themselves had been actively promoting the idea of a railway to Achill a few years earlier. This was quite true, and the shipping service did not become established after all.

In 1899 the Parish Priest at Newport, Revd R. O'Connor, asked the company to consider running a train on Sundays from Mallaranny to Newport to allow people to attend Mass, as there was no church in Mallaranny at this stage. The company initially declined to do this on grounds of cost. Further correspondence took place between clergy in Newport and the company on this subject, and later that year a Sunday service was introduced, operating from Achill to Newport and back. The Archbishop of Tuam wrote a letter of thanks to the company on behalf of his Diocesan 'Tourist and Resorts Committee'. This gives a clue as to why the company had changed its mind: it was considered that the local traffic alone was insufficient to warrant the operation of a train, but during the tourist season sufficient numbers of people on holiday in the area required transport to church services, so the train was operated - during the summer season only. In July 1900, it was restored indefinitely after a gap during the winter and spring, as the company was satisfied with the first season's operation.

Trains such as these Sunday services, which operated over a short section of the line only, were rare on the Achill branch. Neither Newport nor Mallaranny would have required a dedicated service of their own on a regular basis. However, mention is made in the MGWR's traffic minutes in 1900 of a plan to discontinue a connection from the Limited Mail train which operated between Westport and Newport only. This was clearly a short-lived experiment. In addition, with both Newport and Mallaranny having facilities for locomotives to take water, it is possible that livestock specials could have operated to either place from time to time. Newport had ample cattle sidings and loading space at the western end of the station.

In 1904 the company turned down a request for combined rail and hotel tickets at a discount, plus the use of a lecture hall in the Mallaranny Hotel, in connection with a religious convention. Other requests for privileges were agreed to or declined apparently at whim: for example, on one occasion reduced fares were allowed for Newport Races and Achill Regatta, but not for a Regatta at Westport. The Revd T. Boland of Achill arranged for the issue of cheap fares to a sale of work at Achill from as far afield as Castlebar, but a request from the Revd Peter Varden CC for a donation towards a new church in Mallaranny was refused. Perhaps the company saw their meagre Sunday fares income from Mallaranny threatened by Revd Varden's church! However, the company agreed to transport materials to build the church to Mallaranny at half the normal rate, while in the meantime another clergyman, Revd J. Grierson of Achill, had requested 'three or four return passes' to Dublin. This one was declined, along with a similar request

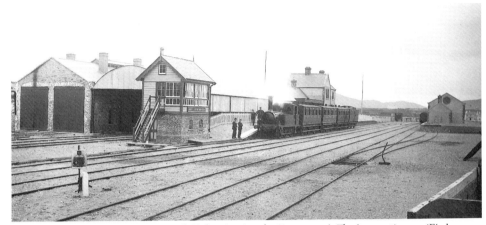

A train awaits departure from Achill shortly after the line opened. The locomotive, an 'E' class 0-6-0, heads a passenger train so typical as to be worth noting: three standard MGWR six-wheeled coaches, a composite, first and third class vehicle in that order, followed by a 'birdcage-roofed' passenger brake van. The MGWR built large numbers of these coaches in the 1880s and 1890s. They were extremely well built, and many lasted in use with CIE as late as the early 1960s, by which time they were decidedly dated! A small number have survived: one may be seen at a hotel in Clifden, Co. Galway, while another (No. 62 of 1892) is retained for preservation by the Railway Preservation Society of Ireland, Whitehead, Co. Antrim.

Lawrence Collection, courtesy National Library of Ireland

Shortly after the line opened, an Achill-bound train hurries downhill from Mallaranny. The earthworks still have little or no vegetation growing on the sides - compare this with the view on page 56, of a train heading in the opposite direction at this location a few years later.

Lawrence Collection, courtesy National Library of Ireland

from Mr Bindon Scott, the owner of the Slievemore Hotel in Dugort, on Achill Island. A road service had been established to connect the Slievemore Hotel with Achill station - this will be referred to later.

By 1906, Revd Varden's church in Mallaranny was complete, and special trains were operated in connection with the Consecration. And at Achill, Mr Patrick Sweeney, Merchant, successfully persuaded the company not only to operate a special train to a sporting fixture there, but also to donate £1 10s. 0d. towards the event. During the early years of the railway fair days and sporting events at Achill Sound and Mallaranny attracted considerable numbers of people from over a wide surrounding area.

In 1900, a deputation of local farmers and businessmen asked the company to reduce charges for the carriage of 'Manure, Seeds, Etc., in large quantities' and livestock. The company promised to consider it in the future. Requests such as this were frequent but rarely led to anything other than a token gesture by the company. The Clerk of Westport Union arranged a special train late one evening in November 1900 to convey 'boys and girls returning from Glasgow'. Special train services for seasonal migrations of farm workers from the Achill area to Britain were to become a regular feature each autumn. Doubtless many of the passengers reflected on the fate of many of their friends and relatives a few years earlier, when the first train to traverse the line had carried their remains back to Achill after the drowning tragedy in Clew Bay.

Travelling conditions were commented on in an unfavourable light in the first few years of the century. In addition to passenger discomfort, the animal rights lobby was active all those years ago: the Irish Society for the Prevention of Cruelty of Animals complained that live fowl were carried in unsatisfactory conditions on trains.

Tourists were now coming into the area, with increases in numbers of 12 per cent in some years. The company's hotel at Mallaranny was attracting a satisfactory number of visitors, allowing the company to offer discounts for travel from Dublin direct to the hotel, which was immediately beside the station. In the month of August 1902 an express train was operated between Dublin and Achill as an experiment to encourage tourism. This was deemed to be successful, and in 1903 the same train operated in July and August on Tuesdays and Saturdays. A similar service operated from Dublin to Clifden, and it is possible that the Achill service was a connection from this train at Athlone. By 1904, September was included as well. This train carried a dining car with it as far as Athlone, which went on to Galway and Clifden. It is not known whether catering facilities were provided on the Achill portion. The MGWR did not have many dining cars, so it is unlikely. However, in 1905 a Mrs Hackett complained to the company of a loss incurred in running the catering services on the 'Tourist Train'. The 'Tourist Express' was not consistently successful, as it was discontinued after the 1906 season.

Another new service for tourists was started in 1908. A train left Achill at 6.35 pm, to arrive in Mallaranny by 7.00 pm. The purpose of this was to carry people to entertainment in the hotel there. The return working was some hours later. The train operated on Wednesdays and Fridays from mid-August until mid-September, and the operation was repeated each autumn until at least 1910. In a further effort to cater for new traffic, and following an annual inspection of the

This extraordinary vehicle was one of the earliest examples of an internal-combustion powered rail passenger vehicle in the world. It entered service in January 1912, primarily to carry mails, but with room for 11 passengers in a somewhat cramped seating area. Never successful, it was withdrawn in 1916 when the Post Office no longer required a mail service on the line. It was used as a track inspection vehicle for some years afterwards, then placed in storage. The picture above shows the vehicle when new, as shown in the maker's catalogue; the lower picture is the only one known to exist of the railcar as used. This picture was taken about 1930 at Inchicore works, where it was in storage. It will be noted that the engine compartment at the front is slightly smaller, and more solid wheels have been fitted by this stage - this followed a rebuild of the car when it was only three years old, in 1914.   *R.N. Clements, courtesy Ernie Shepherd*

line, plans were made to erect a small wooden platform at Moran's Crossing near the point where the railway crossed the Owengarve River between Newport and Mallaranny. This river was well known for good fishing, and the company had bought fishing rights there for the benefit of guests at the Mallaranny Hotel. Depending on the success of this, consideration was to be given to building a permanent station. While it is not recorded whether or not the platform was built, trains did stop there periodically at this time, on request.

The Post Office had started carrying mails by train, but was not satisfied with a service of two trains in each direction per day. The Public Works Office (PWO) asked the company to run additional services, but was told that further services would be unremunerative though it would operate them if somebody else (e.g. the PWO or the Post Office) would pay for them. Not surprisingly, the Post Office contented themselves with existing arrangements. In January 1911, the company had a meeting with the Post Office to discuss new plans for carriage of mails over the line. The Post Office was anxious to have a mail train during the night or very early morning. Clearly, operating such a train would have been of benefit to nobody but the Post Office, and would have been unprofitable. One possible solution was to operate such a service using a light rail motor car rather than a steam locomotive and carriages. The MGWR's Engineer was asked to report on the feasibility of this. He considered the idea to be impractical, but the company decided to order a suitable vehicle nonetheless. In the meantime the Post Office signed an agreement with the company for the provision of one return trip per day using this vehicle. The Engineer made his own suggestions about a suitable specification for a railcar from the firm of Drewry's, but one was ordered from Charles Price & Sons, Broadheath, Manchester, instead. The cost of the railcar was £446, and delivery was to take place within 10 weeks. By December, it had arrived and trials took place. Modifications were made to the brakes, which were found to be unreliable. The car entered service soon afterwards. It had a 27 hp petrol engine, and was reported to be capable of 53 miles per hour, though it is most unlikely that such speed was ever attained in service!

In addition to mailbags, 11 passengers could be carried on tram-type wooden seats in the passenger saloon. The railcar was timed to depart from Westport at 5.35 am, reaching Achill at 7.35 am - no need for high speeds there! Stops were made for passengers or mail at the two intermediate stations as well as at Rosturk, Carrowsallagh and Tonregee for mail only. The railcar was found to be underpowered and a new engine was fitted at the end of 1914 at a cost of £171. But even at this early stage, the Post Office was considering transferring its mail deliveries to road transport, and notice was given to the company in June 1916 that they no longer required this service. Consequently, the railcar was taken out of service and placed at the disposal of the Permanent Way Department for use on line inspections. In this guise it lingered on in occasional use for another few years, based in Dublin. However, it was little used, and was last seen in a derelict state awaiting scrapping at Inchicore works, Dublin, in 1933. By this time, the Midland Great Western Railway had been succeeded by the Great Southern Railways (GSR) for eight years, but the railcar still carried faded MGWR brown livery. So ended the Achill line's one foray into internal combustion territory.

The afternoon Achill to Westport passenger train skirts Bellacragher Bay on its sharp climb up to Mallaranny station, about 1906. The leading coach has the distinctive roof profile of main line stock, and is probably one of three first class coaches of this design built 1905-6. The second coach is a first/third composite, with lavatory compartment in the centre, while the third coach appears to be a four-compartment first. The normal configuration of an Achill train would have had more third class seating than first, and a recently built coach such as the leading one would hardly have been sent as far away as Achill: was this a special train? Had the photographer been called out specially for the occasion? Alternatively, this working could have been related to the 'Tourist Express'.

Lawrence Collection, courtesy National Library of Ireland

Chapter Seven

The Line's Heyday

Before the line opened, businessmen had begun to calculate the potential benefits the railway would bring. Fish merchants from the locality, and from as far afield as England saw the opportunities for through carriage of fish from Achill pier to markets further afield. A Mr Alexander Hector of Birmingham approached the MGWR in June 1894 asking what arrangements could be made to transport fish from Achill when the line was open. The company replied that they couldn't tell him until they got possession of the line from the Board of Works, but that they would do everything possible to help him. Hector submitted plans for a fish and ice store that he wanted to erect at Achill Sound. Eventually a tender from Collens Bros to build it was accepted, and it was finished by March 1896 at a cost of £538. Later, the company gave Hector £5 to provide a small room in the fish store for his foreman to live in! One hopes the unfortunate foreman became used to the smell . . .

By 1900, another Birmingham fish merchant named Smith rented storage space for fish at Achill as well. The Revd Father Flatley wrote to the company asking that they build a new pier near the station, but nothing appears to have been done. Smith then contacted the company asking for a shed to be built to accommodate his wares, and the company offered him a corrugated iron shed 60 ft long for a rental of £10 per year. Smith offered £5, which seems to have been accepted, and the shed was built at a cost of £110.

By now the Achill line had buoyant fish traffic. The railway company was keen to encourage this, as the fish would all be taken to Dublin by train. Between 1905 and 1910 the company paid for repairs to the quay wall and a new slipway to improve facilities for landing catches of lobsters. In addition, it threw its corporate weight behind a campaign by a group of four trawler operators who were preparing a submission to the Government to further improve the pier facilities further. Hector's fish storage and handling facilities also received improvements, and a specially negotiated low rental was agreed between the company and Hector.

Mention has been made of plans at building stage for provision of a station at Tonregee, near Achill. The station was to be a two-storey building with a platform, and would cost £2,980. The station was to cater for fish traffic from the pier nearby, as local fishermen were finding it inconvenient to take their catch to the station at Achill instead. In March 1899 the Revd W.S. Green wrote to the MGWR on behalf of the fishermen, asking for a siding at 'Tonregee Claggan Ferry'. For once, the company readily agreed, providing they did not incur any expense other than the straightforward installation of this siding. No land purchase was necessary, as the company already owned the land adjoining the track on which the proposed station was to be built. The station itself was never built, but the siding was put in place by May 1899, and a path led from here for some half a mile to the sea. Unloading the boats, transport by cart up the pathway, and loading into wagons on the siding was the sole responsibility of the fishermen, as the company did not provide staff here. No sooner was the siding in use than locomotive No. 26 *Britannia* derailed while coming off the siding onto the main line. It is reported that 'serious delay' was caused to a special fish train as a result. The siding may not have been properly completed at this stage, as final Board of Trade approval for its operation was not secured until October 1899. Indeed, the whole operation of the fish siding is rarely referred to in traffic minute books of the period, and it appears that little use was made of it. In 1905, correspondence between the Board of Works and the MGWR suggested that the company had not yet provided rail for the siding. It may be that it was originally laid with temporary rail (a possible cause of the derailment) and nothing had been done since to replace this. Certainly, it appears that the siding was out of use soon after this - perhaps temporary rail was lifted, never to be replaced due to low usage of the siding.

The Congested Districts Board asked the company to install a similar siding for fish traffic near Inishlyre, a few miles outside Westport, but this request was declined, despite detailed plans and surveys having been made for both a pier and a connecting railway line.

One of the more famous Lawrence Collection photographs, taken shortly after the line opened, shows a view of Achill station, with a train in the distance at the platform. It will be seen in this photograph (*page 50*) that there is quite a clutter of builder's left-overs and general debris on the seaward side of the tracks - Worthington left this behind when he finished work. Elsewhere along the line, there were other redundant materials. This came to the attention of the Board in May 1901, when it was reported that local youths had made an obstruction on the track just outside Achill station using a pair of wheels from one of Worthington's wagons, and a large wooden block. Worthington was contacted and told to clear all his rubbish away from the line, but two years later it was still there. Presumably the company cleared it away themselves eventually.

A number of wooden buildings remained at Achill, which had been used as workmen's dormitories during construction. These were in poor repair, but in May 1896 three rooms in one were separated from the others and let to the porter at Achill station. The rest were cleaned, and the operator of the horse and cart service from the station to the Slievemore Hotel on the Achill Island was told not to keep his horses in them any more! As a result, the operator, J. Sheridan, complained to the company, and a 'lean-to' hut was made from old sleepers for his horses - this was let to him for 1*d*. per month.

A feature of the autumn and winter weather in the west of Ireland is the wind. Locomotive crews would comment on the way the wind caught them in the exposed locomotive cabs as they rounded the hill at Mallaranny. An unusual incident at Achill station in October 1900 involved two wagons being blown along a siding they were parked on, during a storm. They came to the points, and were derailed.

The company let a vacant cottage at Achill to a Mr Thomas Sweeney of Belmullet in 1909. This appears to have been one of the dilapidated wooden buildings left over from construction, however the company was able to charge Sweeney 1*s*. 6*d*. per week for it. Despite the temporary nature of these buildings, some 30 years later they were still in use as or stores or even dwellings. In 1924 the MGWR's Engineer described them as being 'in a very dilapidated condition'. and 'quite beyond repair'. Nonetheless, a railway employee was allowed to stay in one he was living in, due to the lack of any alternative accommodation. His house was described as being of galvanised iron, rather than wood - perhaps it was one of the originals with a covering of corrugated sheeting. Only a month later the Engineer had second thoughts about this house - he condemned it as unfit for human habitation and drew up a plan to build a new two-storey house. This was not actually done, so the occupant must have found another home elsewhere. It is likely that the remaining contractor's buildings were demolished at this time.

The cutting sides in Mallaranny, having been altered at the time of the inspection just before opening the line, were clearly not fully satisfactory, as rocks were noted falling off them from time to time. On one occasion just after the line opened, a train was delayed on account of stones falling down onto the track. It is assumed that remedies were made, as no further trouble occurred.

In the light of a spate of minor derailments, the MGWR's Engineer carried out an inspection of the track in 1897. He reported that the original track was too light, and some replacement of the existing rails with heavier ones was carried out.

In 1905, the MGWR purchased four acres of land from Mr Vesey Stoney for use as a ballast pit at Mallaranny. The opening up of this pit involved re-housing 11 of Vesey Stoney's tenants, whose cottages were on the land. A siding was laid into the pit, trailing to the Newport direction, from a point about 300 yards east of the station on the inland side of the main line. The pit was not very big, and it does not appear to have seen much use. However, the remains of the quarrying there may be seen to this day.

In August 1907, a new level crossing was built over the railway at Kilbride, near Newport. A number of families were to be settled there, and the MGWR asked the Congested Districts Board, who were responsible for the rehousing, to provide a gatehouse and gatekeeper.

In December 1914, all railways were put under Government control on account of World War I. No changes took place on the Achill line during this period, but three stables at Achill were rented to the Anglo American Oil Company in 1915. These were used for the storage of petrol supplies in cans. Government control of the railways continued after the war ended, and was extended to the end of 1921. By this stage, Ireland was in the throes of the struggle for independence, and British troops or munitions were being carried throughout the country to engage the insurgents. As elsewhere, railwaymen often refused to operate these trains - drivers would leave their engines when British troops tried to board trains at stations, and so on. In the West of Ireland in particular, the effect of this paralysed many lines. The Achill line was severely affected, and at the end of September 1920 the train service was withdrawn entirely, not being reinstated until January 1921. The boycotting of trains carrying military personnel and equipment was ended in December 1920, but a different dispute now affected the railway. Boilermakers at the MGWR's works in Dublin had gone on strike. This affected locomotive maintenance, and the dispute was not resolved until well into 1921. Disruption to services therefore continued. At one stage the Board considered laying off the entire staff on the Achill line due to inability to resume a train service, but thankfully this did not become necessary.

In March 1915 Westport District Council asked the company to alter a crossing at Gortawarla due to the approach road being too steep. The company refused, on the grounds that the Board of Trade had passed it at the time of the line's opening. Since the line was now open for some 20 years, the company questioned why had this issue not been raised before if it was that serious. The company took no action, and it must be presumed that if any work was done, the District Council did it themselves.

The War of Independence and the Civil War following the Treaty of 1921 are well documented elsewhere, but their effect was felt on the Achill line. No sooner had the Treaty between the British and Irish been signed, and some semblance of normality resumed, than the Civil War broke out. The MGWR's lines in the West were badly hit by disruption to services and damage to locomotives, rolling stock, track, bridges and stations. About two miles on the Westport side of Newport, bridge Nos. 817 and 819 were damaged by explosives on 24th August, 1922. The train service was cancelled again in October for several months. Before repairs were fully completed, bridge 819 was more severely damaged by another explosion on 7th November. A contemporary military report stated that 'The Irregulars principal base is around Newport - breaking roads, bridges, and lifting rails - some trains derailed'. Other bridges in the area and elsewhere were repeatedly damaged by explosives, the attacks continuing over the winter. Locomotives and rolling stock fared no better, with a number of attacks taking place in Achill station itself. On 12th December, 1922 locomotive No. 37 *Wolf Dog*, clearly a regular on the line, was damaged, while a train was derailed in Mallaranny station itself. At Newport, damage to the railway line had to be repaired under military guard. On 10th January, 1923, three locomotives were derailed at Achill after being set off along the line in full steam in the direction of Mallaranny: Nos. 14 and 15, and again No. 37. A driver named Geraghty was ordered to appear before the Board in connection with this derailment. The following day, a plan by the Irregulars to attack two other locomotives was foiled by military intelligence. Two days later, third class coaches Nos. 44, 6 and 78 were destroyed by fire. On 20th January, another two carriages were totally destroyed by fire - first class coach No. 7, and third No. 12. All five coaches were of standard 6-wheel non-corridor type. In May 1923, the Civil War ended, and services quickly were restored to normal.

Political troubles apart, some improvements had been made in Mallaranny station. The hotel manageress received a 50 per cent pay rise (to £125 per year), and after 25 years, more than halfway through the line's existence, the kitchen in Mallaranny station house had a window put into it! £9 was spent in bringing electricity to the station building (the hotel had had it for years), but only the station master's office and the lights on the platform had it installed. Presumably the station master's living quarters remained in the dark ages for some time longer.

Chapter Eight

Mishaps and Incidents in MGWR Days

The first record of any mishap on the line was between Westport and Newport on 5th July, 1894, when locomotive No. 37 *Wolf Dog* failed while hauling a train. It was reported that 'a piece blew out of one of the cylinders', and the train was delayed by 15 minutes. It is interesting to note that this locomotive was in use on the line as early as this, before the line was even open beyond Newport. In the first instance, it was not one of the locomotives originally ordered for the line - maybe there were 'teething troubles' with these? Secondly, *Wolf Dog* had an interesting history. She was one of six engines built as 2-4-0s and used on a variety of services over the MGWR system, but rebuilt at Broadstone in 1899/1900 as the MGWR's first 4-4-0s for use on the Dublin-Sligo line. They were not a success there, and the six 'D-Bogie' class as they were now known, appeared on the Achill line where they took over from the 'E' class tank engines used initially. *Wolf Dog* was thus employed on the line both before and after rebuilding. As GSR No. 533, she survived the closure of the Achill line, was transferred to Athlone, and remained in service until 1953. After 1925, the 'D-bogie' locomotives were officially known as the 'D16' class, but were better known as the 'Achill bogies' on account of their close association with the line.

Following completion of the building works, over a thousand labourers had been gradually laid off, and there is some evidence to suggest that a few of them had grudges against the railway company as a result. Ireland was also in the midst of a period of political unrest, especially in western areas. A number of malicious attacks took place on the railway at this time. These could have been attributed either to politically motivated activities or just to petty criminals. The MGWR's Western Division Engineer reported in August 1894 that an 'outrage' had taken place between Westport and Newport. Four mileposts and three gradient posts had been uprooted from the side of the line and thrown into a river, and large stones were placed on the track at a level crossing nearby. The Royal Irish Constabulary was informed, and a £20 reward was offered for information leading to the apprehension of those responsible. Nobody was caught. In the following month some stones and an iron wedge were placed on the track in front of the 4.05 pm train near Mallaranny. This was potentially much more serious, and the train struck the obstruction. Fortunately it was travelling slowly at the time and only the trailing wheels of the locomotive were derailed. The first reference that clearly identifies one of the 'E' class tank engines built for the line is in September 1894, when No. 115 *Achill* failed near Mallaranny due to a broken piston head while hauling the 10.18 from Westport. In December, a coach came off the track at Newport causing 1½ hours' delay to the 1.35 from Achill. This annoyed some passengers - possibly they missed the connecting train from Westport as a result.

During the winter, further malicious attacks took place. 'E' class locomotive No. 116 *Cong* and coach No. 77 were damaged when they collided with large boulders which had been placed on the track near Newport. A 40 yard length of wire fencing was stolen on the outskirts of Westport in March: the RIC offered a £10 reward for information about the theft. Incidents of this nature were taking place in other areas too, and the company was sufficiently worried to inform the Chief Secretary for Ireland about the problem. In one instance, a shot had been fired through the window of a carriage in Co. Roscommon - luckily, there was nobody in the compartment at the time. After a lull of about a year, a boulder was placed on the track at Achill station in April 1897, but no damage was caused. Two more serious incidents followed in the autumn of 1897. On 26th October, the 1.10 pm train driven by driver J. Byrne, hit a flock of sheep which had strayed onto the line near Newport, killing 14. The owner had left a gate open, allowing them to wander onto the track. On 17th November, shots were fired at the 4.10 train from Achill as it left Mallaranny station, and two windows were broken. A report was made to the RIC, but no culprit was found. There seem to be more reports of straying livestock being killed around Mallaranny than anywhere else, so maybe this had something to do with attempted damage to the railway in this area. In 1900, a youth named Cooney was apprehended as he placed large stones and other objects on the track in front of the 12.00 train.

A number of minor derailments occurred within stations, often caused by carelessness while shunting, such as changing points before a vehicle had fully crossed them. Newport's station master, T. Mc Loughlin, was cautioned after a wagon left the track there, and incorrectly set points caused No. 114 *Stork* to derail at Achill. On Christmas Eve, 1900 a more serious accident was caused in this way. A locomotive, its tender and a coach all came off the rails in Achill station. Station master Boag was reprimanded for not having the station lights lit properly, while driver John Farrell had £1 deducted from his Christmas bonus for not reporting the matter. The train involved was a loaded passenger train entering the station, rather than a shunting manoeuvre and the company received several claims for compensation. A local youth and a nurse from Keel, on Achill Island, were awarded compensation by a Dublin court as a result of the accident.

Elsewhere, crews had to cope with stray livestock from time to time. Driver John Farrell, on the 1.35 pm train from Achill, ran over a cow near Mallaranny in March 1895, but no action was taken against him as it was decided that the owner had been negligent in letting it get onto the track. Mr Clarke of Mallaranny was cautioned after a cow that he owned strayed onto the track in June 1896. Apparently, he had left the gate open, and the unfortunate cow was reported to be 'disabled by a train'. Delays to trains could sometimes be attributed to difficulties in loading livestock onto them - on 4th November, 1896 the 4.10 mixed train left Achill 1¾ hours late, due to delays in loading. This was worsened by a combination of a heavy load and slippery rails due to wet weather. On another occasion, while cattle were being loaded into a train at Achill, the railwayman in charge noticed that two of them had fallen, and he opened the wagon up to investigate. Unfortunately, some of the other animals in the wagon escaped and ran away, one being killed and another injured. The owner successfully claimed compensation from the railway company as a result.

On 12th June, 1896, a more spectacular accident took place in Westport station. A train driven by the same driver Farrell collided with a wagon that had been left sitting on the main line. While Farrell's train was unharmed, the wagon was propelled through the station, left the rails and careered over an embankment near Altamont Street, landing on the roof of a house owned by a Mrs Bridget Brown. The Westport shunter, Thomas Mulcahy, and a guard named W. Brown (no relation!) were held to be liable, had their pay reduced, and were transferred to stations elsewhere. Mrs Brown and her husband were compensated for shock, and damage to their house.

Between Tonregee and Mallaranny, No. 65 *Wolf* and its tender came off the track, halting the progress of the 4.10 pm mixed train from Achill on 10th July, 1895. The signalling system failed on another occasion, delaying the 7.45 am train by 1 hour 20 minutes between Mallaranny and Achill.

On one occasion in 1901, a jaunting car driver named Lavelle and an RIC man suffered injuries while chasing two of Lavelle's horses, which had escaped at Achill station. However, they managed to safely retrieve the horses a ¼ mile up the road. The same Mr Lavelle complained to the company that a railway inspector at Achill station was abusive to him. Nothing was done - no doubt Broadstone had more important matters to attend to than name-calling in Achill station!

There is a record of a boy being killed while playing on the Achill line in 1901. The accident appears to have happened in Achill station, where the youth was hit by a wagon in motion. The victim was the son of driver Blayney. At this time it was common for drivers' sons to follow in their footsteps and join the railway as well. In 1908, a driver named O'Boyle from Mallaranny persuaded the company to employ his son as an 'understudy' for him.

The railway had its share of personnel problems. At Achill, the first station master had allowed the station to become generally untidy, and was inefficient in his clerical duties. He also kept the refreshment room closed. He was given an ultimatum to open this during normal hours, and clean up the station, or he would be replaced. Eventually, after failing to raise standards sufficiently his services were dispensed with. In 1902 his successor was also dismissed for slovenly work, and for failing to keep the refreshment room open, just like his predecessor in 1895! He asked to be re-instated, but the company refused. Irrespective of his work, the new man had been well known and very popular in the locality and local people supporting his case for re-instatement prepared a petition. But a replacement had been appointed, and that was the end of the matter. The MGWR was taking seriously its standards of what is nowadays called 'customer care', and at the same time consideration was given to employing somebody at Mallaranny station/hotel who could speak French - an early foretaste of the considerable boom in European tourism in the area a century or so later.

A spate of disciplinary incidents was recorded at around this time. A gatekeeper at Knockloughra, Mallaranny, had his pay reduced for 10 weeks after he left the crossing gates closed across the track as the 6.55 am train approached. The train, driven by one J. Farrell, hit the gates causing damage to them and to one carriage. Farrell was involved in another incident, after reporting a porter at Achill for changing the points while a carriage was being shunted - the vehicle was derailed as a result. Another porter at Newport was in trouble too in July 1899: he had been fined £1 in Newport Petty Sessions for assaulting a passenger in the station. He was transferred elsewhere, with a warning that if he did it again, he would be sacked. A late night special train, probably a summer excursion, crashed into level crossing gates on 19th August, 1899, due to the man in charge of the gates apparently having forgotten about the extra train. A similar incident happened in December 1901, following which gateman O'Hara (near Achill) was told that if he forgot to open gates again, he would forfeit his house.

Further incidences of vandalism took place in February 1903. One involved a stone thrown through the window of a coach in a passenger train leaving Westport. It is of interest in that it is the first time a bogie coach is mentioned as part of a train formation on the line. The coach in question was No. 40, an 11-compartment vehicle built by the Metropolitan Carriage & Wagon Co. in 1900. The usual train formation on the line from the outset had been three 30 ft six-wheeled coaches plus a six-wheeled passenger brake.

A derailment took place due to speeding in July 1905. As the 4.10 pm mixed train left Mallaranny bound for Achill, it picked up speed running down the long 1 in 70 incline to the west of Mallaranny station. It continued to milepost 20½ where six vehicles left the track. Fortunately, the train remained upright, but it was probably a close escape. Five passengers claimed compensation for minor injuries. The driver was suspended and ordered to appear before the Board to explain himself, after the inspecting Engineer had declared that there was nothing wrong with the track. Accompanying him were the train's guard, two other staff, and station master E.A. Crowley. Crowley explained that the train had started late, and the crew had only been trying to make up lost time. The driver remained suspended for two weeks, and was then re-employed. Less serious derailments continued to happen from time to time: a temporary employee at Achill managed to derail a coach by changing the points while it passed over them, and a porter, also at Achill, did the same, causing £2 worth of damage to the track. The constant recurrence of this problem at Achill was the subject of a visit by the Engineer at one stage, but he found no defect with the track. The reason was doubtless related to the ongoing problems of inefficient management within the station itself. Instances of station masters being disciplined at Achill have already been referred to: in all, the names of three men holding this position were mentioned in records of disciplinary hearings in the first 10 years of the line's existence.

A landslide beside the line caused a delay of 2¼ hours to the 6.40 am train from Achill as it travelled between Newport and Westport on 3rd January, 1907. The length of the delay suggests that efforts were made to try to dig through the obstruction there and then, as no damage is reported to either track or train. A few years later, the same thing happened again in the same place. This time, the 6.40 goods train was affected again, being delayed an hour.

On 27th February, 1909 a major inspection of the line was undertaken. A few days later another derailment (of No. 19) took place in Achill station, due to the signalman's carelessness. Standards had obviously lapsed back to the norm once the Directors' party had moved on!

Water supplies at Newport had been poor in the past, and in 1916 a spare water tank from Claremorris station was re-erected here to 'reduce the need for pumping'.

In 1921, political events led to the creation of the Irish Free State. Over the next two years, resultant unrest caused severe disruption to train services, and between 1922 and 1923 the line was closed completely for several months, before settling down once more to its daily routine.

Chapter Nine

The Great Southern Era

On and from 1st January, 1925, the MGWR became part of the Great Southern Railways. The new Irish Government had been anxious to amalgamate all railways that operated wholly within the Irish Free State, for greater efficiency and economy in working. The GSR was the result, but it remained a private company, not a State controlled one. The only outward sign of change at first was that the trains and stations carried new liveries. Under the MGWR, locomotives had been green, and carriages a mid-brown with yellow lining, though from 1918 carriages were repainted a very dark maroon. In stations, paintwork was finished in a brick red colour and beige. The new company painted locomotives a dull battleship grey, with all the elaborate lining, nameplates and numbers replaced by a standard type of cast numberplate denoting the engine's new GSR number. Carriages remained maroon, though a lighter shade began to appear, bearing the new coat of arms of the GSR. Carriages bearing the GSR's attractive brown and cream main line livery were to be seen from the late 1920s. Station buildings were repainted in green and cream when redecoration became necessary. For eight years, the timetable remained much the same, as described elsewhere. However, the GSR did not have the resources to support unprofitable lines, and the carriage shed at Achill station was taken down in the late 1920s. However, the tracks remained for some years afterwards for storage of spare rolling stock, but were little used. They were eventually removed some years later, shortly before the line closed, as a 1937 photograph of this area of the station shows no trace of tracks where the carriage shed had been. Two short sidings against the buffer stops appear to have been removed at around this time as well, and by 1937 the goods yard run-round loop had also been lifted. The hotel at Mallaranny was renamed the Great Southern Hotel, a name it was to carry until many years after the demise of the railway line which served it.

In 1931, the GSR set up an advisory Committee to report to the Board on the state of a number of unprofitable lines, including those to Killala and Clifden which were eventually closed in 1934. The Achill line was not included in the survey at this stage, but, by the time the report was completed, Achill had joined it along with the Cork & Muskerry narrow gauge system. Initially, it was believed that the line should be kept open, with costs cut by reducing the train service to one per day in each direction. This was because it was felt that replacement road services would lose more money than the railway line, since it was estimated that 25 per cent of the former rail traffic would go to private road transport. The most heavily used trains were the 11.40 am from Achill and the 8.30 pm from Westport - these were to comprise the entire service. The author of the 1931 report also expressed concern about the number of buses that would be needed to carry the farm workers going abroad each season. It was pointed out that it would cost £13 for a bus to travel empty from Dublin to Ballina garage, and on to Achill to collect these passengers before taking them to Westport for the train. With up to six extra buses needed on some spring days, this was considered an unnecessary expense. It was pointed out that when workers were returning to the district, the number of passengers for stations on the line would have to be checked in Dublin before the train left. The bus garage in Ballina would be advised so that they could send a suitable number of extra buses to Westport to meet the train when it arrived in the evening. As time progressed, and the amount of money required to renovate the railway became evident, these objections were overcome, and the financial case for closure became clear following the 1932 Transport Act. This Act regulated the previously undisciplined operation of private road transport services, which had hit the railway so hard in recent times. It also gave the GSR the authority to operate its own road services. It was therefore no surprise that a further report in December 1933 recommended closure of the railway to Achill.

It had been noted by the GSR's Accountant that traffic returns had diminished in recent times, and in July 1933 he wrote to Mr Considine, the station master at Achill, asking for an explanation, thus:

To: Agent, Achill and Westport
Dublin, 20th July, 1933

On looking over your passenger returns I notice that there is a large falling off in the passenger traffic booked between the stations Westport to Achill and intermediate, as compared with the Traffic booked in the previous years, viz., 1930 and 1931.

Be good enough to look into and say if you can give me a general idea as to the cause of the Decrease. You are not to take into account traffic booked to Stations beyond Westport, such as Castlebar. It is only purely Branch Stations you are to deal with.

Hartnell Smith
Accountant's Dept.
(Audit Section)
Broadstone

Considine, and his counterpart in Westport, replied that the Irish Omnibus Company had recently commenced an Achill-Westport-Ballina bus service, and that this was taking may of the passengers that formerly travelled by train. For an Achill islander who had previously had to pay 10 shillings for a car to drive them to Achill to catch the train, it was now cheaper to go by bus to Westport than to go by car to Achill. Considine also pointed out that for the last two years, the Thursday market train had not been operated due to cuts in the train service. From the Westport end, it was felt that the severe economic depression in the area at the time was also to blame.

In fact, comparison of traffic figures for the years 1930 and 1932 gives a clear idea of the impact that road transport was beginning to have on the railway.

	1930	1932
Passenger fare receipts	£1,653	£610
Goods receipts	£2,196	£995
Cattle traffic receipts	£208	£71
Train miles operated*	36,058	16,576
Maintenance costs:		
Track, Signals, Operating	£6,716	£3,155
Locomotives and rolling stock	£617	£309
Overall net loss in operating the line	£3,458	£1,573

* By 1932, the service had been reduced.

The total income generated by the line had dropped by more than half in the two year period. The equally dramatic drop in operating costs gave a temporary respite - the reports for both years repeated that the track had little useful life left, and considerable expenditure would be needed in the near future. With the economies in costs reducing but not eliminating the loss, and the prospect of expenditure of some £11,000 per year on track for the next four years, it would have been necessary to show a clear potential for a vast, and permanent, increase in traffic. Clearly, no amount of investment would have guaranteed this.

Preparations were made to close the line six months later, from 1st June, 1934. The locomotive shed at Achill had one track lifted so that a bus could be stabled inside overnight, and fuel tanks for a bus and a lorry were installed at a cost of £125. A garage was built in Westport to house the bus that would replace passenger services. It was estimated that a 20-seater bus would cost about £1,000, and a lorry £3,560. The cost of these would be covered by annual savings made as follows:

Locomotive crews & coal	£1,285
Track, signalling and station costs (buildings maintenance and wages)	£1,584

The County Council objected, saying that the road was unsuitable for the replacement bus and lorry traffic, especially beyond Mallaranny, where the existing road was not metalled. The GSR deferred the closure date to the end of 1934, when the Ballina-Killala line was due to close also. Opposition mounted, with local businessmen petitioning the GSR to leave the line open. Two businessmen from Achill Sound headed a large deputation travelling to Dublin to meet the Minister of Industry & Commerce, Sean Lemass. They had spent considerable time and effort in researching and compiling statistics to make a case for the retention of the line, with all station masters on the line giving their full co-operation to the project. The station staff at Achill gave them a rousing send off, fog detonators having been placed along the line in front of the train. At Mallaranny they were received by the station master (Mr Forbes), and joined by a local publican. They had a similar send-off from the staff there, more fog signals exploding as they left. When they arrived in Dublin, Theckla Beere, Secretary to Lemass, received them. The politicians met them with a blustering attitude, and Theckla Beere pointed out that they only had time to listen to hard facts. But facts they got! The Committee had done their homework thoroughly. Mr W.J. Sweeney of Achill Sound presented their case, quoting figures that showed traffic levels increasing in almost every area. Cement was now being brought into Newport by rail, and proposals for the carriage of turf by train were being made. The Ministerial party had no choice but to agree that the figures were correct, and compliment the delegation on their research. However, Lemass summed up the case for the forthcoming closure by pointing out the financial difficulties the GSR was in. He said that arrears of maintenance would cost some £40,000 to bring the line up to insurable condition, and that the company was left with no choice but to discontinue services.

Some other last minute efforts were being made to try to keep at least part of the line open. Canon McDowell of Achill had led a deputation to the

In the following selection of 12 photographs, we embark on a return journey over the Achill line. We follow in the footsteps of the famous railway traveller and photographer, Henry Casserley, who took the following pictures on 17th and 18th July, 1934, the last summer before the cutbacks which eventually led to the line's closure.

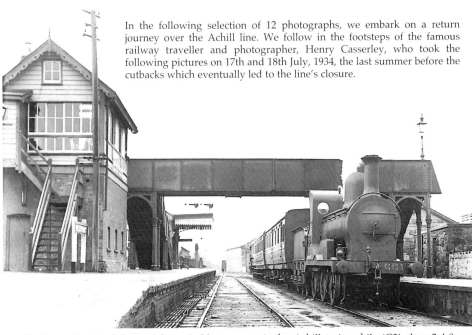

Having arrived in Westport from Dublin, we await the Achill train while 'G2' class 2-4-0 locomotive No. 651 prepares to take the 6.00 pm Night Mail to Dublin. The locomotive has a full head of steam, and it blows off noisily. The light load of this train will be added to as it wends its way east, and at Mullingar it will link up with the Mail from Galway. By five minutes to midnight, these two carriages will form but part of the cavalcade entering Broadstone station in Dublin.

The way ahead: view from the carriage at Mallaranny as the weather becomes dull.

Achill station, 17th July, 1934, locomotive shed on left, with wagon of locomotive coal in front. It will be seen that there is a smoke stain above the left-hand doorway only - the right-hand side of the shed had not been used for some time, and was used to park the bus which carried passengers from 1935 onwards. The two tracks in the foreground were formerly covered by the carriage shed, but were largely disused by this stage. Despite these signs of the line's decay, a healthy level of good traffic is shown by the number of wagons on the extreme right, adjacent to the goods shed.

Next morning, we find ex-GSWR 'D17' class 4-4-0 No. 57 as our train engine for the run back to Westport. No. 57 was drafted in to work the line by the Great Southern. With a tender loaded with coal, she is being turned to face Westport on the turntable at the eastern end of Achill station.

No. 57 eases off the turntable. The passenger van and carriage can be seen behind the signal box awaiting the locomotive. The fireman for the day, seen standing on top of the tender, is Peter Clynes of Athlone, and the man on the ground is Mick Maher, a locomotive cleaner from Westport.

Having picked up the carriage, No. 57 reverses into the goods yard to attach eastbound wagons to the back of it. The passenger van has been shunted to the other end of the carriage.

No. 57 awaits departure at Achill with the 11.40 am train to Westport. This was the 'mixed' train - on account of generous time taken to shunt wagons at the two intermediate stations, the train will be allowed 2 hrs and 2 mins to travel the 27 miles to Westport. A 16 minute stop is made at Mallaranny, while at Newport the train will wait for 34 minutes - shunting first, then waiting to pass the 1.00 pm train in the other direction. The afternoon train, by comparison, took 1 hr 15 mins to make the same journey - this time with no wagons.

Just after midday, 18th May, 1934. A glorious sunny afternoon beckons, as No. 57 pauses for water before drawing forward into the platform. Plenty of time for passengers to enjoy the view. The climb to Mallaranny has not taxed the engine as we have a light load - steam blows off vigorously.

General view of Newport station facing Achill, the morning train to Westport has arrived, and
there is more shunting to be done. This must be completed before the 1.00 train to Achill arrives
in the other platform in about half an hour.

The carriage waits at the platform while the locomotive has run-round to the other end of' the
train to attach wagons bound for Dublin. The lightweight construction of the track is evident, as
is its worn condition. This was to prove a major factor in plans to close the line, which were
being formulated even as this picture was taken. Once shunting is complete, No. 57 must await
the arrival of the Achill bound train in the other direction before she can leave. There are only
two people on the other platform awaiting the Achill train - on a glorious sunny morning, it is
unlikely that the waiting room contains many more.

Newport station - detail of footbridge, looking towards Mallaranny - signs of neglect are already evident in the paintwork. In the distance, the locomotive detaches two wagons from the train.

Eventually, 'Achill Bogie' No. 534 (ex-No. 2 *Jupiter*) ambles into Newport with the 1.00 pm train to Achill. The entrance to Newport tunnel can he seen behind the train. We may now resume our leisurely journey to Westport.

Department of Industry and Commerce opposing the closure plans on the grounds that turf traffic from local bogs was in the process of being developed, and that the roads were in no fit state to carry buses and lorries. He met the Traffic Manager of the GSR in September 1934, but it was to no avail. The GSR representative assured him that the company was committed to providing the area with satisfactory public transport, and outlined the comparative costs of establishing a road service as compared with the relaying of the railway line. He pointed out also that the line was losing £4,000 a year - a slight exaggeration if traffic figures are examined, but in broad principle it was correct. The Canon had no choice but to accept this, and indeed expressed his 'thorough satisfaction' with the statistics put to him.

Newport traders and businessmen presented a petition to M. Kilroy, their TD, who took the matter up with the company. He was replied to along the lines that the GSR actually hoped to improve public transport in the area through provision of buses and lorries.

But one possible lifeline was still open to the railway. Under a recent Government initiative, incentives were provided for people in poorer areas in the West of Ireland to harvest turf (peat) and send it by train principally to Dublin. In other areas, the railway made arrangements for transport of turf to suitable railheads where it would be loaded onto trains. Already, small quantities of turf were being loaded at Achill, and it was suggested by various local people that the tonnage being taken away by train should increase dramatically - one estimate was that Achill would produce 10-15,000 tons in 1934. Out of 21 other locations in Ireland where turf might be loaded, this was the highest figure, with many other locations having an estimate of 3,000 tons. The state of the roads was again cited as a reason to keep the railway, if only to cater for this traffic. One internal memo within the company in 1931 went as far as to say that the replacement road service might cost more to run than the train services as things stood, and that the addition of turf traffic would increase the difficulty in transferring to road haulage. But this report, the author of which is unclear, only succeeded in having the issue postponed. In 1934, when total closure was looming, it was proposed that the line be left open at least as far as Newport, for turf traffic only.

But the road from Westport to Achill was still not capable of dealing with regular road traffic, so the GSR was persuaded by Mayo County Council to keep the line open for a while, on the understanding that it could be closed once road improvements were carried out. Therefore, from 31st December, 1934 a bus service replaced the passenger trains, while the railway remained open for the heavier goods traffic, including the turf. The Achill line had won a reprieve - but the writing was clearly on the wall. The track was almost life expired - a 1930 report had indicated that between Westport and Mallaranny it only had a life of six years left, while beyond Mallaranny it would only last three years. An overall speed limit of 25 miles per hour was applied, with 20 mph over the section from Mallaranny almost as far as Tonregee. Only the lightest classes of locomotives were allowed over the line. By April 1935, the roadwork was still not finished, and Mayo County Council succeeded in persuading the GSR to re-instate the passenger train service temporarily, though it was not widely advertised to the public. A year later work was still not finished and the passenger train service made an official re-appearance in the timetable from 20th April, 1936. In the meantime, the turf issue arose again. The Turf Development Board (TDB) wrote to the GSR to ask for 50 per cent of the cost of laying a siding beside the line to load turf at Meenacloghafinney Lodge, a remote district some half a mile north of the line between Newport and Mallaranny. Should the GSR agree, the Turf Development Board claimed they would ask the Government to pay the other 50 per cent. Hardly surprisingly, the GSR replied to the effect that while they did not object in principle, they were not in a position to provide funding. As it happened, the TDB's estimates of 20,000 tons of turf annually proved to be hugely excessive - in 1935 the Achill line carried a mere 978 tons. Following a meeting between the GSR's Traffic Manager, P.J. Floyd, and representatives of the turf industry, it was agreed by all that the GSR's lorries could adequately cope with any turf traffic on offer.

But the line was now living on borrowed time, and in January 1937 Lemass announced that the line would definitely close completely as soon as the road was ready. At a late stage, another attempt by the turf industry to have the railway kept for turf traffic only, and as far as Newport only, fell on deaf ears. To be fair to all concerned, it would not have been a viable proposition to keep the line for this traffic alone, especially as annual tonnages had not quite lived up to expectations. In August 1937 GSR officials travelled to Mallaranny and Achill to plan redundancy terms for staff and other matters relating to the closure. Already, unused sidings and the goods run-round loop at Achill were being removed, and a small pile of rails lay to one side of the station. Some interesting traffic statistics which were prepared at the time are dealt with in *Appendix Two*, but it is interesting to note in summary that most of the goods coming onto the line was destined for Achill, while most of the outgoing goods left Newport. Livestock traffic at Mallaranny and Achill had dwindled, and the bulk of the remaining traffic related to Newport, where three fairs typically loaded about 20 wagons each. Newport was handling a quantity of cement traffic, as a Westport merchant imported it into the Quay there. But Westport Quay was busy as well - it is interesting to note that much of the goods traffic that left Achill was bound for Westport Quay. Mallaranny station was overall the least busy, both in terms of passenger and goods traffic.

However, one unexpected and tragic event upset the gradual progress towards closure. It was customary for many local people to migrate seasonally to Scotland to work on farms there harvesting potatoes. Harvest workers would travel in groups, often requiring special trains leaving Achill at 6.00 am, to connect with the first train of the day from Westport to Dublin. They would then take the boat to Scotland, where they would stay in dormitory accommodation on the farms they worked on. On 17th September, 1937, a fire broke out in one such dormitory, at Kirkintulloch, near Glasgow. The dormitory was locked, and 10 boys from the Achill area aged between 13 and 23 were tragically burnt to death. The bodies of the victims were taken to Dublin in preparation for another funeral train over the Achill line, 43 years after the first. So great was the sense of shock and tragedy in the community that the local Westport enginemen did not feel able to drive this train, and an Athlone based

CROAGH PATRICK PILGRIMAGE, 25th and 26th JULY.

As set out on Posters the fares by the Special Trains, on Saturday from Broadstone and on Sunday from Athlone, Ballinrobe, Limerick, Galway, Sligo, Achill, and Ballina, will include Bus from Westport to Croagh Patrick and back and tickets will be combined Two-Piece. Bus Dept. will collect Outward portion. The combined fare for children 3 to 14 years will be half the Combined Adult fare plus one shilling.

Stations are to requisition direct from Audit Office the supplies of Special tickets required.

The usual Summer Tickets will also apply to Westport and such passengers, should they visit Croagh Patrick, will be charged local Bus fare by Omnibus Dept.

Extract from GSR employee's circular, 18th July, 1936. Arrangements were being made for collection of fares from passengers on special trains to Westport (from a number of locations including Achill), from where a bus connection brought passengers to the holy mountain.

H.C.A. Beaumont Collection

This is the only known photograph showing the goods yard area of Mallaranny station, looking towards Achill. Several wagons await unloading at the goods shed. The two tracks in the centre are the two goods sidings, while the two tracks on the far right are the main running line and the loop. Mid 1930s.

J. Macartney Robbins

Above right: The locomotive crew of No. 530, pictured on the last public train about to leave Achill for Westport on Thursday 30th September, 1937. *From left to right:* Hughie Kenny (locomotive cleaner), fireman Paddy Blaney and driver Pat Dawson. All three were based at Westport.

Frank Dawson

Right: The final farewell, Achill, 1st October, 1937. The station master, Mr Considine, shakes hands with the driver of locomotive No. 530 as she prepares to leave Achill for ever. The locomotive had arrived to clear empty wagons the day after the line closed.

J. Sweeney, Achill Sound

'D16' class locomotive No. 530 at Achill locomotive shed, 1st October, 1937. Standing beside the engine is Mr Considine, the station master. The locomotive was working to clear empty wagons following the final withdrawal of train services the day before. *J. Sweeney, Achill Sound*

crew was drafted in. The driver was Paddy Currivan, and the fireman Ed Murphy. The train consisted of 'D16' class No. 534, hauling four vans. As the train left Dublin, word had spread across Ireland, and at many stations along the way large numbers of people appeared to pay their respects. A contemporary newspaper reported that 8,000 people waited at the North Wall in Dublin where the boat from Scotland was to dock. Blinds were drawn in houses across Ireland in respect for the dead. The first stop was at Mullingar, where 1,000 people had gathered at the station. The newspaper reported their shock at the spectacle of the survivors, one or two men and '19 sad-faced young girls returning home with the dead bodies of their brothers and cousins'. One man sat in isolation in the corner of the carriage, having lost all three of his sons. When the train reached Athlone, the survivors were given a hot meal in the station restaurant, and again a large crowd turned out to offer their sympathy.

It was dusk as the train left Westport, and on account of the poor condition of the track, and the sensitive nature of its load, the train proceeded along the Achill line at 15 miles per hour. The train stopped at Newport, where 'the Very Revd McDonald led the people present in a recitation of the Rosary'. By the time they arrived at Achill, it was dark and the signal cabin had been closed. One thousand people were present at the station to meet the train, and the 10 coffins were removed and placed in the Parish Church overnight, before interment in Kildownet Cemetery on the island, in a special plot that can be seen to this day. Following harrowing scenes as the bereaved relatives of the victims took delivery of their remains, special arrangements were made for the locomotive to run round its train before returning empty to Westport that night. With only two weeks to go before the line closed, locomotive facilities at Achill were being run down, and the locomotive had loaded up with coal at Westport in order to have enough for the return journey, as the crew had been told none would be available that night in Achill.

Local people remembered the drowning tragedy of 1894 and the fact that trains had carried coffins over the line both at its inception and at its closure - Brian Rua O'Cearbhain's deadly prophecy had been fulfilled. A bizarre postscript to this took place three years later, when the bus service that had replaced the railway itself encountered a tragic incident near Achill. The bus was stopped by a rope across the road between the two parapets of a bridge: sadly, a mentally ill person had hung himself on the bridge.

On Thursday 30th September, 1937, 'D16' class locomotive No. 530 hauled the last 4 o'clock train out of Achill, watched by Mr Considine, the station master, and a number of staff and local people. The locomotive was crewed by driver Pat Dawson, fireman Paddy Blaney, and a cleaner named Hughie Kenny, all based at Westport. By 10 pm that night, the last incoming train had slipped into Achill station - there was no hurry now, the line was closed forever.

Chapter Ten

Train Services

The first train services on the section just as far as Newport started on 1st February, 1894. The service provided for passenger trains was as follows:

		am	pm			am	pm
Westport	dep.	10.18	4.05	Newport	dep.	8.25	2.05
Newport	arr.	10.41	4.28	Westport	arr.	8.48	2.28

There were no intermediate stations or stops. The journey time of 23 minutes gave an average speed of just over 20 mph, though with allowances made for starting and stopping times the running speed would have been around 25 mph. No complete details are to hand regarding the alterations to the service once trains started operating through to Mallaranny (on 16th July), but it is likely that two trains per day were provided in each direction as before. It is probable that a separate goods train operated a return trip as well, as reference was made at the time to the carriage of mails by a train at 6 am. This would have allowed a locomotive to travel from the Westport end to Newport, in order to take the first passenger train of the day into Westport. Newport never had a locomotive shed, though it did have facilities for engines to take on water, so it is unlikely that a locomotive was based there even at an early stage. If no goods train had operated out to Newport earlier in the morning, there would have been no locomotive at Newport to take the first train of the day, the 8.25 am, back to Westport. Similarly, in the afternoon, when the last train arrived back at Newport at 4.28 pm, a balancing working would have been necessary - possibly mails were taken back to Westport at this stage.

The exact details of the first timetable to Achill have not survived, but it is known that two trains were provided, the first in each direction carrying both passengers and goods, and the second carrying passengers only. The following gives an idea of the original train service (weekdays only):

May 1895	Mixed	Passenger		Mixed	Passenger
	am	pm		am	pm
Westport	10.40	3.56	Achill	6.55	1.35
Newport	11.10*	4.29*	Mallaranny	7.20*	1.55*
Mallaranny	11.50*	4.55*	Newport	7.50*	2.20*
Achill	12.13 pm	5.10	Westport	8.28*	2.50*

The 6.55 from Achill connected with the morning train to Dublin (Broadstone) at Westport, enabling the traveller to arrive in Dublin at 9.30 pm - over 14½ hours later! The morning train that left Dublin at 9.15 connected with the 3.56 to Achill, so the journey back to Achill took some 8 hours. The reason for this apparent discrepancy was that the journey up to Dublin involved several lengthy stops awaiting connecting services - probably at Westport and Athlone. A third train that ran at least on Fair Days, and every day in summer

* Approximate times: actual advertised times not known.

eventually augmented this service. In the early years, this train left Achill at 4.10 pm. No Sunday service was provided either on the initial Newport timetable or at the opening to Achill: all the above services operated Monday to Saturday only.

Alterations were made soon after the start of the service, doubtless in the light of experiences in actual operation. For example, the 10.40 train from Westport was retimed to leave there at 10.18, and the 3.56 departure in the afternoon was changed to 4.05 and then 4.10 pm, running now as a mixed train, following requests from the public.

The earliest full working timetable for the line that survives is that which was effective from 1st May, 1897. The service was as follows, weekdays only.

		1st, 2nd & 3rd class	Mixed	1st, 2nd & 3rd class			1st, 2nd & 3rd class	1st, 2nd & 3rd class	Mixed
		am	pm	pm			am	pm	pm
Note		1	2	3			4	5	6
Westport	a.	9.28		3.51	Achill	d.	6.40	1.10	4.10
	d.	9.33	1.30	3.56	M'ranny	a.	7.02	1.32	X 4.39
Newport	a.	9.54	X 1.59	4.17		d.	7.04	1.34	4.54
	d.	9.56	2.14	4.19	Newport	a.	7.31	X 2.01	5.31
M'ranny	a.	10.23	2.51	X 4.46		d.	7.33	2.03	5.46
	d.	10.25	3.01	4.48	Westport	a.	7.54	2.24	6.15
Achill	a.	10.47	3.30	5.10		d.	8.00	2.25	7.00

X = Trains cross here

Notes
1. From Castlerea (dep. 7.30).
2. From Westport only.
3. Depart Dublin (North Wall) 8.05 a.m., and Dublin (Broadstone) 9.15 am.
4. Arrived at Dubin (Broadstone) 2.45 p.m., with a connection on to arrive at Dublin (North Wall) at 3.10
5. Arrived at Dublin (Broadstone) at 9.30 p.m. No onward connection.
6. Mixed train Achill-Westport only. From Westport to Dublin the train operated as Goods only. Arrival at Dublin (North Wall) at 10.39 pm.

It will be noted that the 1.30 pm mixed from Westport crossed the 1.10 passenger train from Achill at Newport, and the 3.56 pm passenger train from Westport crossed the 4.10 pm mixed train from Achill at Mallaranny.

The above train service involved a locomotive plus coaches based in Castlerea running through to Achill on the first down service of the day. It is probable that this set returned as the 1.10 pm passenger from Achill. The 6.40 am train from Achill doubtless formed the 1.30 pm mixed back to Achill. In this case, another locomotive and set of coaches must have been available at Achill to form the 4.10 pm departure.

Revision of the timetable was carried out in 1898 to improve connections with the up and down Limited Mail trains between Westport and Dublin during the tourist season. Few other details of early changes to the service on the Achill line survive, but the basic pattern of two to three trains per day in each direction was maintained for most of the line's life.

Few timetables survive for the first 20 years of the century, but the basic service as already described continued virtually unaltered. The 1911 timetable (weekdays only) is the only surviving example to show more than three departures from each end per day, though one in each direction was seasonal. This was as follows:

Distance M. ch.			Mixed am	Ltd Mail am	Passenger am	Passenger† pm
0	Dublin (Broadstone)	dep.	*	7.00	9.15	
160.74	Westport	arr.	9.39	11.45	4.01 pm	
		dep.	9.55	11.55	4.06	6.50
168.60	Newport	dep.	10.32	12.15 pm	4.27	7.10
179.32	Mallaranny	dep.	11.15	12.48	4.54	7.36
187.46	Achill	arr.	11.40	1.10	5.15	7.58

Distance M. ch.			Passenger am	Mixed# pm	Passenger pm	Passenger† pm
0	Achill	dep.	6.40	12.25	4.00	5.30
8.14	Mallaranny	dep.	7.04	1.00	4.54	5.53
18.62	Newport	dep.	7.33	1.28	5.42	6.19
26.32	Westport	arr.	7.54	1.49	6.09	6.38
		dep.	8.00	2.03	6.20	
187.46	Dublin (Broadstone)	arr.	2.15 pm	7.12	§	

* This train originated in Castlerea (dep. 7.10 am)
† 1st June to 30th September only.
\# Mail train from Westport.
§ To Castlerea only arr. 8.18 pm.

No mention is made of Sunday trains, so it must be assumed that they had either been withdrawn for good at this stage, or were of such a temporary nature that they were not considered to be worthy of inclusion in the published timetable.

The 1920 timetable (weekdays only) for the line is the next survivor. It shows the general pattern of service that was to continue on the line almost until closure. By this stage no mention is made of seasonal tourist trains. Three trains per day were provided, as shown. By this stage, it was possible to work the service with just one locomotive based at Achill and another working through from the Westport end.

Distance M. ch.			Mixed am	Ltd Mail am	Passenger pm
0	Dublin (Broadstone)	dep.		7.25	1.30
160.74	Westport	arr.		1.04 pm	7.47
		dep.	8.00	1.09	7.57
	Carrowsallagh Crossing	call	8.08		
	Rosturk Crossing	call	8.11		
168.60	Newport	arr.	8.30	1.28	8.16
	Newport	dep.	8.45	1.29	8.17
179.32	Mallaranny	arr.	9.29	1.54	8.42
		dep.	9.44	1.58	8.44
	Tonregee Crossing	call	10.15		
187.46	Achill	arr.	10.20	2.18	9.05

Distance M. ch.			Ltd Mail am	Mixed pm	Passenger pm
0	Achill	dep.	10.50	3.30	6.00
	Tonregee Crossing	call		3.44	
8.14	Mallaranny	arr.	11.12	3.59	6.22
		dep.	11.15	4.14	6.24
18.62	Newport	arr.	11.42	4.58	6.51
		dep.	11.44	5.13	6.53
	Rosturk Crossing	call		5.27	
	Carrowsallagh Crossing	call		5.30	
26.32	Westport	arr.	12.05 pm	5.38	7.15
		dep.	12.15	6.00*	
187.46	Dublin (Broadstone)	arr.	6.20	12.15 am	

* Limited mail to Dublin.

An interesting feature of this timetable is that it shows one train in each direction booked to stop at several level crossings, as well as the stations. These stops were not publicly advertised, and appeared only in a footnote in the Working Timetable for the use of the railway's employees. They probably dated from the period of railcar operation - mails were being set down here between November 1911 and January 1916. By 1920 the railcar service had finished, and for several years afterwards ordinary service trains called at these places. No station facilities were provided, the train just stopping on request to pick up or set down. By 1924, these stops had been deleted, officially at any rate, though it is believed that unofficial stops may have been made for a time afterwards. A curious error in timetabling is evident here, and is indicative of the casual and localised nature of many such temporary stops, on country lines in general. Rosturk and Carrowsallagh are between Newport and Mallaranny, not Newport and Westport. A train leaving Westport at 8.00 am, as above, could be expected to reach these places some minutes after 8.45, the time at which it left Newport - not in advance of its 8.30 arrival there. It must be assumed that the times given for arriving and departing Newport were slightly awry as a result, as extra time was allowed between Westport and Newport, rather than Newport and Mallaranny, for these stops!

By the 1920s road competition was beginning to make its presence felt, despite the fact that the road from Westport to Achill was still unsurfaced and bus services were many years away. Economies were made throughout the MGWR system and the 6.00 pm passenger train from Achill and its return working at 7.57 were dropped from the timetable by June 1921.

However, these trains were restored a few years later, and instead the first train in each direction was altered to run on Thursdays only for Achill Market Day. This set a pattern for the train service that became standard with few alterations until 1931. As a typical example for this period, we can take the service offered from 1st July, 1928 (weekdays only) as an example:

A rare view of the eastern end of Mallaranny station, late 1920s. On a sunny afternoon the Westport-Achill train coasts into the station with a full head of steam at about 2 pm. The locomotive is No. 534, one of two of the class which received a new larger boiler in GSR days. The leading carriage is not native to the line - it is a six-wheeled third class coach of Great Southern & Western Railway origin.   *Irish Railway Record Society*

At Westport - ready to leave for Achill. The driver takes a last look behind him as No. 535 pulls away from the platform, bound for Achill. The train consists of two ex- MGWR six-wheelers and a passenger brake van. This picture dates from the early 1930s.   *Irish Railway Record Society*

Distance			Passenger Th. O	Ltd Mail	Passenger
M. ch.			am	am	pm
0	Dublin (Broadstone)	dep.		7.10	2.30
160.74	Westport	arr.		12.45 pm	8.17
		dep.	10.45*	12.55	8.25
168.60	Newport	arr.	11.05	1.15	8.45
		dep.	11.06	1.30	8.46
179.32	Mallaranny	arr.	11.31	2.00	9.11
		dep.	11.32	2.15	9.12
187.46	Achill	arr.	11.52	2.40	9.32

Distance			Mixed Th. O	Mixed Th. X	Passenger Th. O	Passenger
M. ch.			am	am	pm	pm
0	Achill	dep.	8.45	11.40	12.25	3.30
8.14	Mallaranny	arr.	9.09	12.04 pm	12.45	3.53
		dep.	9.24	12.20	12.46	3.55
18.62	Newport	arr.	9.49	12.45	1.11	4.20
		dep.	10.05	1.17	1.17	4.21
26.32	Westport	arr.	10.25	1.37	1.37	4.41
		dep.		1.45†	1.45†	#
187.46	Dublin (Broadstone)	arr.		7.20	7.20	

Th. O - Thursdays only. Th. X - Thurdays excepted.
*   From 1st July, 1929 this service ran earlier, leaving Westport at 7.50, and arriving at Achill 8.57 am.
†   This was the Limited (or 'Day') Mail.
#   It was possible to travel on to Dublin, if you had plenty of time to spare! The Night Mail left Westport at 6.00 pm, arriving in Broadstone at 11.55 pm.

The only crossing necessary with this pattern involved the 12.55 from Westport passing the mid-day train from Achill at Newport. As will be seen above, this was normally a passenger train, but on Thursdays it ran mixed, with over half an hour allowed in Newport station. This indicates the necessity for considerable shunting operations in connection with the fair day's cattle traffic.

Again, it was only necessary to have one locomotive stabled at Achill, and this pattern continued for the rest of the line's existence, except for a period in 1934/5 when only goods traffic was carried. During this time a Westport locomotive worked out to Achill and back with the one daily goods train.

Between 1929 and 1931, the 12.25 (Thursdays excepted) departure from Achill and the 11.40 (Thursdays Only) mixed were run to the Thursday timings every day, with the early morning train becoming passenger only.

When the MGWR had been amalgamated with other companies to form the Great Southern Railways in 1925, little change had taken place to train services on the Achill line. However, by 1931, with costs continuing to rise, the GSR turned its attention towards making economies in train crewing costs. As far as Achill was concerned, this meant the reduction of the service to two trains every day, with no extra service on Fair Days. By 1930, the track was deteriorating, and it was estimated that between Mallaranny and Achill it only had a few

The early afternoon train accelerates away from Mallaranny towards Achill in September 1934. The locomotive is No. 535 (formerly No. 3 *Juno*), and the carriage is 175M, the same vehicle photographed by Henry Casserley on his visit that year. The six-wheeled passenger brake immediately behind it is of interest, in that it is clearly painted in the main line livery of brown and cream, rather than the all-over maroon that such vehicles normally appeared in at the time. A horse box, two cattle wagons and another old passenger brake complete the train.

J. Macartney Robbins, courtesy Irish Railway Record Society

No. 531 (formerly No. 25 *Cyclops*) pauses at Mallaranny on a wet day in the 1930s. She is bound for Westport with the afternoon passenger train. On this day no passengers are in evidence at this, the least busy station on the line. The water tower behind the locomotive is still in existence.

Irish Railway Record Society

years' life left in it. A few years later, this led to a speed limit of 25 miles per hour being applied over the whole line, and for a four-mile stretch west of Mallaranny a limit of 20 mph was imposed. Prior to this, less severe restrictions had in fact been in place for many years: overall, 25 mph with very short stretches of 20 mph just outside Westport, Newport and Mallaranny.

Until the end of 1934, the service was basically as follows, still with no Sunday trains provided. The following example is from the 12th September, 1932 working timetable; the two midday services crossed at Newport:

		Mixed	Pass.			Mixed	Pass.
		am	*pm*			*am*	*pm*
Dublin (B'stone)	*dep.*	7.20*	2.40	Achill	*dep.*	11.40	3.30
Westport	*arr.*	12.55 *pm*	8.04	Mallaranny	*arr.*	12.04 *pm*	3.53
Westport	*dep.*	1.00	8.24		*dep.*	12.20	3.55
Newport	*arr.*	<u>1.18</u>	8.45	Newport	*arr.*	<u>12.47</u>	4.22
	dep.	1.35	8.46		*dep.*	1.21	4.23
Mallaranny	*arr.*	2.05	9.13	Westport	*arr.*	1.42	4.45
	dep.	2.20	9.14			†	#
Achill	*arr.*	2.45	9.36				

*   This was the Ltd Mail from Dublin. 'Mixed' relates to Westport-Achill only.
†   Connected with 1.45 pm passenger train to Dublin, arriving Broadstone 7.15 pm
    and Dun Laoghaire Pier 8.25 pm.
Onward train to Dublin at 6.00 (Night Mail), arriving Broadstone 11.55 pm.

On the 31st December, 1934, further economies resulted in all passenger services being withdrawn from the Achill line. From then until April 1935, there was but one goods train per day, which left Westport at 7.45 am, arriving at Achill at 9.45. This was revised in March 1936 to run 35 minutes later. The return working left Achill at 11.15, arriving back in Westport at 1.15 pm, in plenty of time to link up with the afternoon goods train from there to Dublin. A bus service from Achill to Westport and Ballina commenced on 31st December, 1934 with three departures each way between Westport and Achill. The journey took just over 1½ hours by bus, compared with a typical timing of 1 hour 12 minutes by passenger train, or 1 hour 45 minutes by mixed train.

In the meantime, the local authorities were anxious for a railway passenger service to be re-instated to take traffic off the adjoining road while it was upgraded to be suitable for buses and lorries. From April 1935, one return passenger train was provided, along with the goods train and from 20th April, 1936 the GSR restored a service of two trains per day as before. Timings were much the same, except that the 11.40 from Achill now left at 11.10, and the 3.30 pm from Achill left at 4.00 pm. One other change in the last months of the line's existence was that the traveller to Dublin no longer arrived in the old Broadstone terminus: from 18th January, 1937 this was closed to passengers, and trains were diverted to arrive at Westland Row station, now called Pearse station.

This was to be the final timetable arrangement for the line: some 18 months later, at the end of September 1937, the line was closed for good. Replacement buses took over again, running to similar times as the 1934-6 service.

In addition to regular services, special trains were operated over the line, as traffic demanded it. It is believed that in early years at least, special cattle trains were operated in connection with fairs, particularly at Achill, but no details have survived of specific workings. When seasonal harvest workers were on their way to Dublin each year to catch the boats to Britain, special trains would leave Achill early in the morning carrying passengers and their extensive luggage to Westport, where another train would take them onwards. In the 1920s, Mayo made several high profile appearances in Gaelic Athletic Association (GAA) games, and some details have survived of special trains in this connection. On one occasion, a train left Achill at 10.05 am for Claremorris, where it turned north and headed up the line to Collooney, before arriving in Sligo at 2.30 pm having served every station along the way. The return working left Sligo at 7.45 pm, and again served every station the whole way back to Achill, which it reached at nine minutes past midnight. On 8th May, 1926, a GAA special ran as under, with the train having run empty out to Newport in advance:

		am			*pm*
Newport	*dep.*	11.50	Balla	*dep.*	7.00
Westport		12.13 *pm*	Manulla Junction		7.08
Islandeady		12.25	Castlebar		7.18
Castlebar		12.36	Islandeady		7.28
Manulla Junction		12.48*	Westport		7.40
Balla	*arr.*	12.55	Newport	*arr.*	8.00

* Tickets checked here

A connection was made at Manulla Junction with a train from Ballina. Another GAA special operated on 21st May, from Achill to Castlerea, Co. Roscommon and back. An empty train had worked out to Achill in advance, with sufficient coaches for the GAA fans, but another three were added to be left at Achill. This was to allow the timetabled trains leaving Achill to be strengthed for the carriage of harvesters. The special operated thus:

		am			*pm*
Achill	*dep.*	11.15	Castlerea	*dep.*	7.45
Mallaranny		11.33	Westport		9.36
Newport		12.00 *noon*	Newport		9.56
Westport		12.25 *pm*	Mallaranny		10.25
Castlerea	*arr.*	2.15	Achill	*arr.*	10.45

Specials such as this involved much advance planning, and the staff circulars would advise in advance what special staffing arrangements were necessary, and where locomotives and rolling stock were to be positioned in advance, and serviced on the day. However, sometimes everything did not go according to plan. On 25th September, 1932, Mayo played in the All Ireland final, and a special train left Newport at 5.50 in the morning, reaching Dublin at 11.36. The train started from Newport with two bogie carriages and a van, and further carriages plus a dining car were added at Westport. By the time the train reached Dublin, with other carriages having been added along the way, there were 605 people on board - a heavy load by any standards. On the way home, the train left Dublin at 6.35 pm, five minutes late. By the time it had reached Athlone it was running 15 minutes late, and it arrived in Claremorris one hour late. Westport was reached at 1.28 the next morning, rather than the booked time of 11.32 pm, and the last revellers stepped off the train in Newport at 2.10 am, or 2¼ hours late!

It will be noted that two of the trains mentioned above started from Newport, and did not serve Mallaranny or Achill. In 1925, another such special which did originate from Achill had actually left there empty, not taking on its first passengers until further along the line. This is a very telling reflection on local conditions, and may be connected with the fact that the vast majority of seasonal harvest workers travelled from Achill, not Newport. The fact was that on the days these specials ran, the majority of the able bodied people of Achill were out of the country working on farms elsewhere.

No. 530 waits with a full head of steam for departure, Achill, 1937. This photograph is believed to be of the last working out of Achill on 1st October, 1937, which was a train clearing empty wagons the day after the line closed.   *J. Sweeney, Achill Sound*

MGWR 'E' class 0-6-0 tank locomotive, of the type used to provide the original services to Achill. No. 110 *Bat* was used to haul the first train to Achill until replaced by the 'D16s'. No. 110 *Bat* was used to haul the first train to Achill. She was built by Sharp, Stewart & Co. in 1891 and withdrawn in 1955, by which time she had been moved well away from her home territory to the Waterford and Tramore line. In 1953, she hauled a special train to celebrate the centenary of that line.

Irish Railway Record Society

Chapter Eleven

Locomotives and Rolling Stock

As has already been mentioned, no conventional locomotives or carriages were ever built specifically for the Achill line. However, from time to time both were provided with the Achill line, among others, in mind. The only item of rolling stock ever constructed specially for the Achill line was the small railcar, for carrying mail and passengers, which is mentioned in Chapter Six.

When the opening of the line was imminent, the MGWR took delivery of 16 0-6-0 tank locomotives, which were designated as the 'E' class. These locomotives were intended to be used on the lines to Achill, Killala, and Clifden in the West, and on the Kingscourt and Athboy branches elsewhere. Early mention of any specific locomotive on the Achill line usually refers to one of these engines, and it was No. 110 of the class, named *Bat*, that pulled the first train to Achill. These locomotives monopolised traffic for just six years, as from 1901 the six 'D-bogie' class 4-4-0s took over. They were to be seen subsequently on various parts of the MGWR system. Like all passenger locomotives on the MGWR system, they were originally painted in lined emerald green. After 1913, the MGWR painted all locomotives black, lined in red. Twelve of the 'E' class survived into Great Southern, and later Coras Iompair Eireann (CIE) ownership, and were re-classified as the 'J26' class and renumbered. At this stage they lost their MGWR livery and nameplates, and were gradually painted in the GSR's overall battleship grey livery. Like many other locomotives under GSR ownership, their use spread to other parts of the railway system as far from the Achill line as it was possible to be. By 1920, a ban had been placed on six-coupled locomotives traversing the Achill line, a ban that was to remain in place until the line closed. Consequently these locomotives were not to be seen at Achill again. Three ended up on the former Waterford and Tramore line (Nos. 553, 555 and 560), others were to be seen on the former Dublin and South Eastern line on suburban trains, while they were also used for shunting and light duties in Kerry and Cork. The last three survivors lasted until the end of steam traction on CIE at the end of 1962, and were withdrawn in 1963. Details were as follows:

Original No.	GSR/CIE No.	Name (until removed after 1925)	Date built	Date withdrawn	Built by
106	551	*Lark*	1891	1954	Kitson
107	552	*Robin*	1891	1963	Kitson
108	553	*Swallow*	1891	1955	Kitson
109	554	*Fly*	1891	1955	Sharp, Stewart
110	555	*Bat*	1891	1955	Sharp, Stewart
111	556	*Wasp*	1891	1956	Sharp, Stewart
112	557	*Hornet*	1892	1959	Kitson
113	558	*Gnat*	1892	1960	Kitson
114	559	*Stork*	1892	1960	Kitson
115	560	*Achill*	1894	1963	Kitson
116	561	*Cong*	1894	1959	Kitson
117	562	*Moy*	1894	1963	Kitson

Wolf Dog at Broadstone, Dublin, in the early 1900s. This engine was a regular on the Achill line. The ornate lined green livery can be appreciated in this shot. As built, it was numbered 37, but was renumbered three times between 1922 and 1925. Just before the amalgamation, it carried the numbers 35 (1922) and 6 (1924), before becoming 533 under GSR auspices a year later. This was the last of this class of engine to survive: she was broken up in 1953.

The late H. Fayle, courtesy IRRS/Ernie Shepherd

Tractive effort:	11,690 lb.	*Coal capacity:*	1¼ tons
Weight:	33 tons 12 cwt	*Water capacity:*	580 gallons*
Boiler pressure:	150 psi		500 gallons†
Wheel arrangement:	0-6-0T	*Cylinders:*	15 in. x 22 in.
Wheel diameter:	4 ft 6 in.		

* Locomotives buit by Kitson, Leeds.
† Locomotives buit by Sharp, Stewart & Co., Manchester and Glasgow.

Next came the 'D-bogies', which were the MGWR's first bogie engines, but were not brand new. They had been rebuilt at Broadstone in 1900/1 from the six members of the 'D' class of 2-4-0s that had originally been built by Beyer, Peacock & Co. of Manchester in 1880/1. The rebuilt locomotives were intended for use on the Sligo line, but were found to be underpowered for this purpose. In addition, crews reported that they were poor steamers. All six worked for most of their life between Mullingar, Athlone and Achill as a result. Their close association with the Achill line led to their being known as the 'Achill bogies' or 'Mayo bogies'.

In 1900, No. 37 *Wolf Dog*, as a new engine, was turned out in a new livery for the Sligo mail trains. This was an experiment, and it was applied soon after to the 'Tourist Express' to Galway and Clifden, this whole train being painted in the new style. It was deemed to be a success, and the repainted engines and carriages drew many admiring glances. Midland engines had traditionally been emerald green, with black and white lining, while coaching stock was what one contemporary writer called 'a rather nondescript shade of brown'. The new livery, which it was intended to extend to all locomotives, was a medium blue with black and white lining. Carriages were painted to match, with blue lower panels and white upper panels, lined in gold. Contemporary reports claim that this new livery looked very well, but the MGWR took the view after just a few years that it did not wear as well as the old livery. Since the majority of the company's locomotives and carriages still carried the traditional livery, blue locomotives and carriages were gradually repainted as before, though the green was now a slightly lighter shade. *Wolf Dog* became a regular performer on the Achill line, and is mentioned in traffic minutes as having visited the line as a 2-4-0 before her 1900 rebuild, and as a 4-4-0 after that.

Various alterations were made to the class over the years - two were given GSR design 'X' boilers, while Nos. 2 and 3 were superheated. In 1925 when the MGWR became part of the GSR, they were classed as 'D16' or '530 class' and renumbered as shown in the accompanying table. All six survived the closure of the line, and were transferred to Athlone. From then on they were used between there and either Westport or Ballina, taking a connection of the mail train from Dublin. No. 532 was based in Ballina for many years, and ended up eventually as a stationary boiler at Broadstone locomotive shed, Dublin, until the late 1940s. No. 533 worked a variety of trains over the Midland system, including cattle trains - a duty for which it was unsuitable due to its light weight and lack of power - before being broken up, as the last survivor of the class, at Broadstone in 1953. Another member of the class was often to be seen in the 1940s at Westport or Ballina, stored out of service awaiting the attention of a

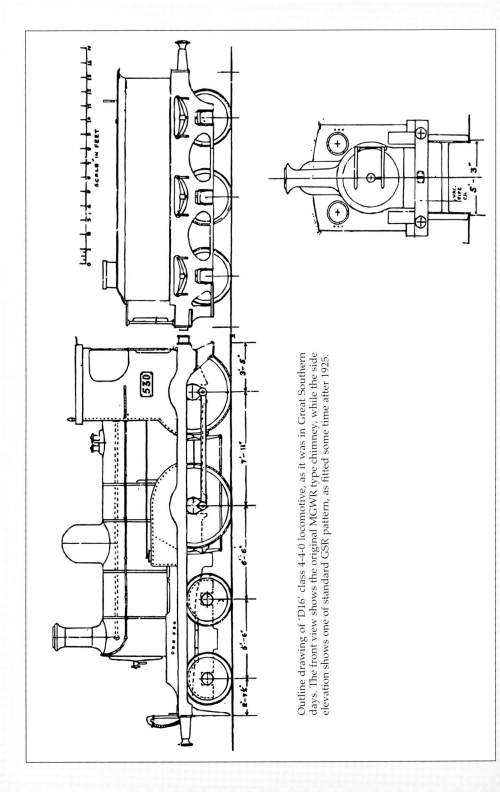

Outline drawing of 'D16' class 4-4-0 locomotive, as it was in Great Southern days. The front view shows the original MGWR type chimney, while the side elevation shows one of standard GSR pattern, as fitted some time after 1925.

A view of an 'Achill Bogie', or 'D16' class locomotive. No. 530 was pictured on Westport turntable in July 1934. Just over three years later, this locomotive was destined to haul the last train out of Achill. Here, she carries her original chimney, replaced by a standard GSR-pattern in photographs in 1937.   *H.C. Casserley, courtesy R. Casserley*

'D16' class No. 530 on Westport turntable in 1934. Behind is a MGWR goods locomotive. The names of the crew members are not recorded.   *H.C. Casserley, courtesy R. Casserley*

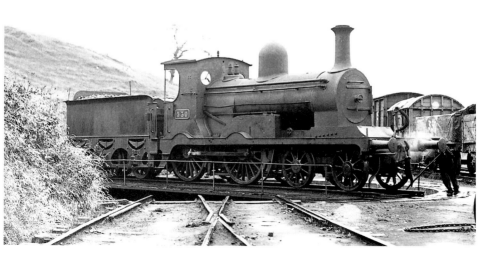

A classic view of an 'Achill Bogie'. Midland Great Western No. 26 *Britannia*, as renumbered 532 by the Great Southern Railways, outlived the Achill line by 12 years, ending her days as a stationary boiler to supply steam in Broadstone works. She is pictured here at Broadstone in the 1940s.   *Author's Collection*

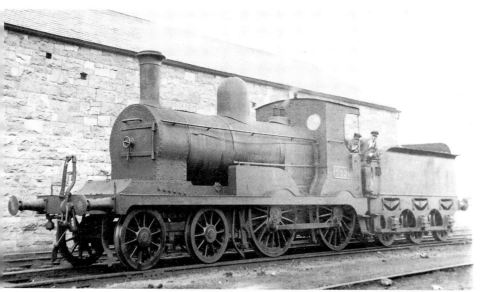

'D16' No. 532 at Westport, early 1930s. While based on the Achill line this locomotive used to work through to Claremorris where it would spend the day shunting before returning with the evening train. However, out of the six members of her class, No. 532 was notorious for the weakness of her brakes, so much so that when she was used for shunting, a brake van had to be attached to the locomotive to provide extra brake power. She was withdrawn in 1949.

Irish Railway Record Society

'D16' No. 531, following rebuilding by the Great Southern in the 1920s. This picture may be contrasted with that of No. 532 (*above*). A larger tender has also been provided.

Irish Railway Record Society

No. 2 *Jupiter*, built 1881 by Beyer, Peacock & Co., Manchester. Renumbered 534 by the GSR, she remained in use on the Achill line until closure, and elsewhere until being scrapped in 1949. She is pictured at Achill about 1910-1915. *Ernie Shepherd Collection*

Ex-MGWR 'G2' class 2-4-0 No. 651 prepares to leave Westport with the 6.00 pm mail train to Dublin on 17th July, 1934. No. 651 was built at Broadstone, Dublin in 1894 as MGWR No. 17 *Reindeer*, and survived until 1959. The engine still carries the distinctive Atock-designed 'flyaway' cab roof - unpopular with crews, as it gave little protection from the weather. The leading coach, of classic Midland Great Western design, carries the Great Southern's attractive brown and cream livery of the late 1920s/mid-1930s period. *H.C. Casserley, courtesy R. Casserley*

fitter from Dublin. In the 1940s, one based at Athlone was used occasionally on the former Great Southern and Western (GSWR) line from Portarlington to Athlone, despite this normally being a duty allocated to a former GSWR locomotive. Details of these locomotives were as follows:

Original No.	GSR No.	Name*	Date built†	Date wdn	Built by	Boiler psi#	type	Cylinders inches
2	534	Jupiter	1880	1949	Beyer, Peacock	160	X	17 x 24§
3	535	Juno	1880	1949	Beyer, Peacock	150	530	17 x 24§
25	531	Cyclops	1880	1945	Beyer, Peacock	160	530	16 x 22
26	532	Britannia	1880	1949	Beyer, Peacock	150	530	16 x 22
¶ 36	530	Empress of Austria	1881	1949	Beyer, Peacock	160	X	15½ x 22
37	533	Wolf Dog	1881	1953	Beyer, Peacock	150	530	16 x 22

*   Until removal after 1925.
†   Rebuilt in 1900/1901.
#   In GSR days.
§   After 1918/1919 rebuild.
¶   No. 36 originally sported a 'flyaway' cab roof of Atock's design. This was later replaced with a conventional type.

Tractive effort:	11,260 lb.	Weight:	40½ tons
Wheel arrangement:	4-4-0	Driving wheel diameter:	5 ft 8 in.

Other locomotives were used on the Achill line. Until the mid-1920s, the 'K' class 2-4-0s made regular appearances, and in fact two of them were recorded as having been damaged at Achill in 1923 during the political unrest of the period. There were 20 of these locomotives, and they had a remarkable history. In the 1870s, the company had taken delivery of a batch of 2-4-0 tender locomotives from the Glasgow firms of Neilson's and Dübs. During the 1890s, 20 were 'renewed', or totally rebuilt, by Broadstone works, emerging back into traffic as the 'K' class. They were soon to be seen on mail trains on the main line to Galway, and also on the Mayo and Sligo portions of these trains. With the exception of one locomotive which was destroyed in 1923, the remainder survived until the mid-1950s. After 1925, the GSR renumbered them and classified them as the 'G2' class. Several of the class lasted until the 1960s, two holding out until the end of steam on CIE. By the time they were finally withdrawn they were the last 2-4-0 tender locomotives on main line passenger duty in the world, and the only locomotives of this type ever to be superheated. They were regarded as an excellent design, and a great tribute to Martin Atock, their designer.

While they were used all over the MGWR system, and therefore were not immediately associated with Achill, there are frequent references to the class appearing on the line. They were stronger locomotives than the 'E' or 'D-Bogie' class, and would have been usefully employed on cattle specials or other uncharacteristically heavy traffic. It is believed that after 1926 they would have been seen at Achill less often, due to many of the class taking up residence on the Sligo line. Details were as follows:

Ex-Great Southern & Western Railway 'D17' class No. 57 takes a breather on arrival at Westport. These locomotives were built by the GS&WR at their Inchicore works, Dublin, between 1883 and 1890.   *H.C. Casserley, courtesy R. Casserley*

Far from its native territory, ex-GS&WR 'D19' class No. 5 awaits duty at Westport in July 1934. These locomotives were occasional visitors to the Achill line after 1925. When track conditions allowed only the lightest engines, they had to be brought in from as far afield as necessary. Locomotives of this class were more usually associated with lines in the South West of Ireland, particularly the Mallow-Tralee line. Just as the MGWR's 'D16s' became known as 'Achill bogies', these locomotives were known as 'Kerry Bogies'. They were Ireland's first 4-4-0s, built at Inchicore between 1877 and 1880. The 'D19s' were the forerunners of the 'D17s', and were the first Irish locomotives to have a leading swing-link bogie. Crews reported them to be lively, but easily winded by a heavy load. Several remained in traffic until the early 1960s, some 80 years after their introduction.   *H.C. Casserley, courtesy R. Casserley*

Original No.	GSR No.	Name	Date built	Date wdn	Boiler psi	Boiler type	Cylinders inches
13	659	Rapid	1893	1961	150	650	17 x 24
14	650	Racer	1893	1959	160	Y	17 x 24
15	660	Rover	1895	1959	160	Y	17 x 24
16	651	Rob Roy	1895	1959	160	Y	17 x 24
17	661	Reindeer	1894	1959	160	Y	17 x 24
18	652	Ranger	1893	1954	160	Y	17 x 24
19	653	Spencer	1894	1963	160	Y	17 x 24
20	*	Speedy	1896	1923	160	Y	17 x 24
21	662	Swift	1896	1955	150	650	17 x 24
22	663	Samson	1896	1959	160	Y	17 x 24
23	664	Sylph	1896	1961	150	650	17 x 24
† 24	665	Sprite	1897	1959	150	650	17 x 24
27	666	Clifden	1897	1957	150	650	17 x 24
28	654	Clara	1897	1963	160	Y	17 x 24
29	655	Clonsilla	1897	1961	160	Y	17 x 24
30	656	Active	1898	1957	150	650	17 x 24
31	667	Alert	1897	1957	160	Y	17 x 24
32	668	Ariel	1898	1959	160	Y	17 x 24
33	657	Arrow	1898	1961	150	650	17 x 24
34	658	Aurora	1898	1954	150	650	17 x 24

*   No. 20 did not survive into GSR days, as she was destroyed in 1923 during the 'Troubles'.
†   No. 24 was the first of 12 of the class to be superheated, following reboilering in 1918.

Tractive effort:	13,870 lb.	Weight:	37½ tons
Wheel arrangement:	2-4-0	Driving wheel diameter:	5 ft 8 in.

After 1925, while the former MGWR 'E' class were no longer used on the line, engines from elsewhere came to the Achill branch. By this stage, the condition of the track was such that all but the lightest classes of locomotives were banned from the line, so any suitable engine was welcome. The former Great Southern and Western Railway's 'D17' class 4-4-0s were to be seen on the Achill line, and one (No. 57) was seen on the line in 1934, still in original condition with GSWR style double smokebox doors. Twenty of these locomotives had been built between 1883 and 1890, and their specification was as follows:

Wheel arrangement:	4-4-0	Weight:	39 tons 1 cwt
Built:	1883-1890	Driving wheel dia.:	6 ft 7 in.
Built by:	GSWR, Inchicore	Boiler:	52/X
Tractive effort:	10,920 lb.	Locomotive Nos.	1, 3, 4, 9, 11, 12, 14, 16
			16, 18, 20, 52-59, 97-98

One other locomotive is worthy of note. While Worthington was engaged in building the line, he used a small tank locomotive on construction trains. The locomotive was an 0-6-0 saddle tank, built by the Hunslet Engine Co., Leeds, in 1889. It was un-numbered, and carried the name *Newmarket*. Worthington obtained it for use on the Newmarket to Banteer line in Co. Cork, which he was currently building. On completion of this project, he brought the engine to Westport, and used it until the Achill line was complete. It will be recalled that

Great Northern Railway (Ireland) No. 204 at Portadown, Co. Armagh about 1930. This engine was built for R. Worthington in 1889 for use on the construction of the Newmarket-Banteer railway in Co. Cork. It carried the name *Newmarket* which it kept when it was transferred to Achill. Upon completion of the Achill line, Worthington used the locomotive elsewhere before selling it to the GNR, who rebuilt it in the form shown. It was used in public service until 1930, when it was withdrawn and scrapped.

Irish Railway Record Society

on the occasion of the Achill drowning tragedy, special arrangements had to be made to enable the train to traverse the as yet unfinished part of the line beyond Mallaranny. There is some evidence to suggest that a contractor's engine may have been used to haul the train on the very last leg of its journey. If that was the case, it is this locomotive that would have been used. On completion of the Achill line, the locomotive was set aside at Newport station for a few years. In 1903, Worthington took the engine to Co. Armagh where it was used in the construction of the Castleblayney, Keady and Armagh railway between 1904 and 1910. Following this, he sold it to the Great Northern Railway (Ireland), which rebuilt it as a side tank locomotive, carrying the name *Mullingar* and the No. 204. It re-entered service as such in 1913, and was withdrawn and scrapped in 1930.

Needless to say, no diesel trains ever operated over the line. While diesel trains were already in use elsewhere in Ireland, particularly on narrow gauge lines, the GSR had no funds available to develop them for routes such as the Achill line. The railway remained steam worked to the end. However, there was the one very interesting experiment with a railcar, already mentioned, carried out by the MGWR in order to satisfy the requirement by the Post Office for a train service early in the morning to carry mails on the Achill line.

The carriages used on the line were originally all of the standard MGWR pattern - 30 feet long, and six-wheeled. All stock was compartment type, with no toilets provided, and gas lit. A typical passenger train would consist of a first class coach, a composite coach, and a third class coach, trailed by a 'birdcage'-roofed brake van. On mixed trains, goods vehicles would be added on to the end of the train. By 1903, bogie carriages were appearing on the line - there is a record of one having a window broken by a stone outside Westport at that time. In later years, with passenger numbers not living up to expectation, shorter trains became the norm, and by the 1930s a typical formation was but one coach plus a passenger brake van. In later years, bogie coaches were introduced, and a typical train formation became one of these plus a van. After the amalgamation, it is possible that carriages of GSWR origin appeared on the line from time to time, but MGWR-type vehicles were very much the norm.

Carriage livery on the MGWR was an all-over mid-brown, lined out in pale yellow. This looked well on a newly painted vehicle, but was reported to become somewhat dull after a time. In 1901, the company experimented with a new livery of royal blue with white upper panels, and gold lining. This livery was applied to selected main line coaches, and the Dublin-Galway-Clifden 'Tourist Express'. This livery looked better than the old one, but apparently did not wear well, and it was discontinued after a few years. Thereafter, the company reverted to the brown livery until 1918, when a very dark shade of claret was applied to carriages as they became due for repainting.

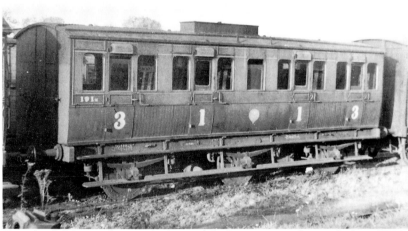

Typical Achill line coaching stock: this coach had an interesting history. Built in 1894, it started life as a second class vehicle, before being upgraded to first class in 1914, and first/third class in 1940, in which guise it is seen here, in storage in Dublin some years after the Achill line had closed. However, it provides a good illustration of the classic solidly built MGWR six-wheeler, the mainstay of passenger accommodation all over its territory for some three-quarters of a century.   *Irish Railway Record Society*

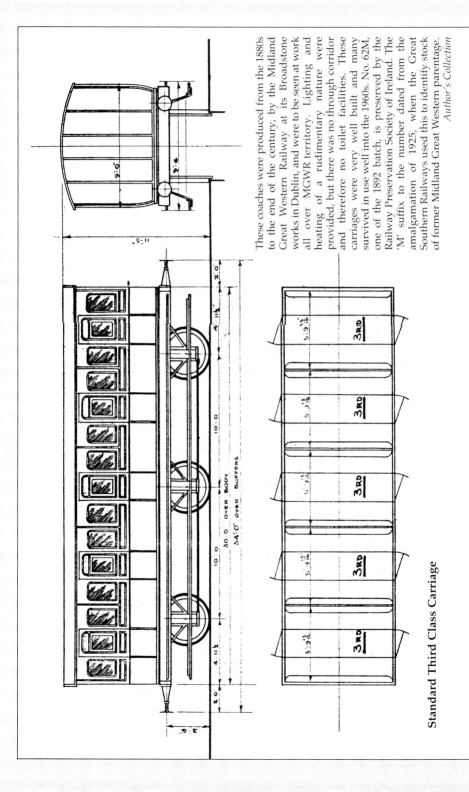

These coaches were produced from the 1880s to the end of the century, by the Midland Great Western Railway at its Broadstone works in Dublin, and were to be seen at work all over MGWR territory. Lighting and heating of a rudimentary nature were provided, but there was no through corridor and therefore no toilet facilities. These carriages were very well built and many survived in use well into the 1960s. No. 62M, one of the 1892 batch, is preserved by the Railway Preservation Society of Ireland. The 'M' suffix to the number dated from the amalgamation of 1925, when the Great Southern Railways used this to identify stock of former Midland Great Western parentage.

Author's Collection

Standard Third Class Carriage

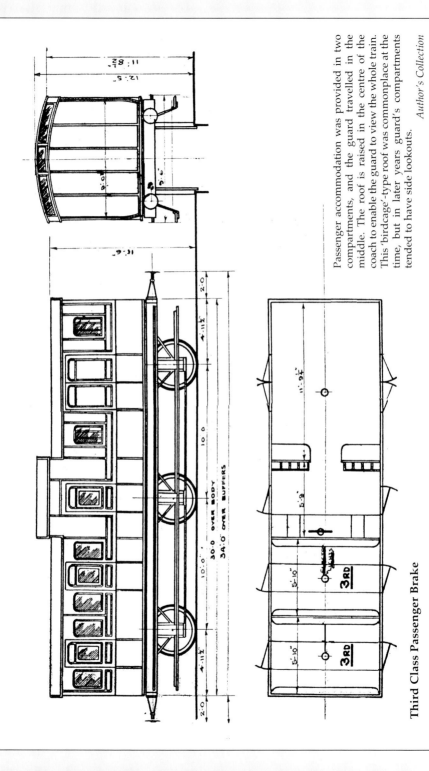

Passenger accommodation was provided in two compartments, and the guard travelled in the middle. The roof is raised in the centre of the coach to enable the guard to view the whole train. This 'birdcage'-type roof was commonplace at the time, but in later years guard's compartments tended to have side lookouts.

Author's Collection

Third Class Passenger Brake

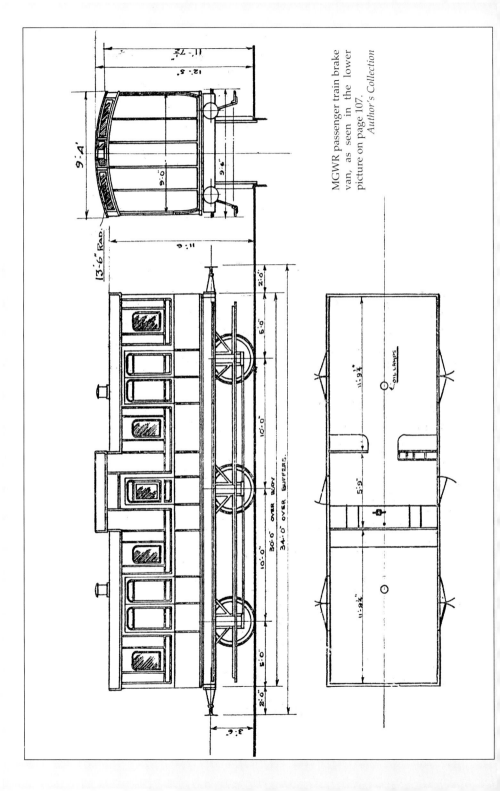

MGWR passenger train brake van, as seen in the lower picture on page 107.
Author's Collection

Ex-MGWR brake third coach No. 10M, of late 1880s vintage, in the 1930s. Oil lighting is still in use in the two passenger compartments in this vehicle. The paintwork is very work-stained - the dark maroon livery has faded into a nondescript reddish-brown, with the lettering and GSR crest barely visible. The coach to the left is a matching first/third class composite coach of similar vintage. *Irish Railway Record Society*

The passenger portion of the afternoon train from Westport, 17th July, 1934. The leading vehicle, in Great Southern Railways maroon livery, is a former Midland Great Western passenger brake van dating from the 1880s or 1890s. This type of vehicle was a standard type of brake vehicle on the line throughout its existence. The passenger coach, in GSR main line brown and cream livery, is No. 175M. This vehicle was one of three composite coaches built for main line use in 1903. It was later converted to an all-first class coach, but in 1931 it became a composite again, carrying first and third class passengers on the Achill line. Note the destination board on the carriage roof, carried through from Dublin. It reads: 'BROADSTONE-WESTPORT-ACHILL'. Apart from Henry Casserley's luggage, there are few signs of life.

H.C. Casserley, courtesy R. Casserley

A long way from home - this wagon of former Dublin & South Eastern Railway ancestry had
travelled to Achill in July 1934. Pictured at Achill.   *H.C. Casserley, courtesy R. Casserley*

Similarly, these two vans were pictured on the seaward siding the same day. Not only did ex-
Great Southern & Western wagons find their way to Achill, its locomotives did too - as seen in
photos of No. 57 on the Achill line the day H.C. Casserley visited.

H.C. Casserley, courtesy R. Casserley

After the GSR took over in 1925, coaches gradually changed to GSR livery. Initially, a dark shade of maroon, not unlike the MGWR's final livery, was applied to coaching stock, but before long main line bogie vehicles were repainted chocolate brown with cream upper panels, while six-wheeled and secondary line vehicles continued to carry the maroon livery. On the Achill line, the inclusion in the train of a main line bogie vehicle would bring the brown and cream livery to Achill, while the brake vehicle was inevitably maroon. After 1935, the GSR introduced a lighter shade of maroon, similar to that used by the LMS in England. At first this was applied to the new steel-panelled coaches on the Dublin-Cork line, but gradually it spread to other stock. However, the brown and cream was still to be seen well into the late 1930s, and photographs taken by the noted photographer H.C. Casserley in 1934 show a vehicle in this livery at Achill.

Regrettably, no MGWR locomotives have survived into preservation. However, two standard MGWR six-wheeled coaches still exist, but in an unrestored state. One may be seen at the premises of the Railway Preservation Society of Ireland, at Whitehead, Co. Antrim, and the other is placed outside a hotel in Connemara.

Goods rolling stock on the Achill line was, like in most places in Ireland, a very mixed bag. As well as MGWR stock, wagons from other companies would occasionally be worked through to Achill with cargoes from afar. After 1925, 'foreign' wagons became more frequent, and when Mr Casserley visited Achill in 1934, there were no less than three wagons of non-MGWR origin present in the goods yard. The MGWR painted wagons a dark grey colour, which changed to a lighter shade under GSR ownership.

Standard Midland Great Western Railway 6-wheeled third class coach, in use as a departmental vehicle in the late 1970s. Long after the Achill line closed, carriages of this type were to be found elsewhere, and this was one of the longest survivors, remaining in traffic until the early 1960s. Shortly after this picture was taken, this vehicle (No. 62) was privately purchased and donated to the Railway Preservation Society of Ireland, in whose Co. Antrim premises it is now protected from further deterioration. *Author*

Chapter Twelve

Road Services

During the life of the Achill line, various road services were operated in conjunction with train services, particularly during the tourist season. When the line was closed, replacement road services were also necessary.

For some time before the advent of the railway, the Slievemore Hotel at Dugort, on Achill Island, had been welcoming the first intrepid visitors to Achill's then relatively unknown scenic delights. The journey to Dugort was by long car, a four-wheeled horse-drawn vehicle common in the West of Ireland at the time. The car may have been long, figuratively speaking: so was the journey. The road from Westport was little better than a stony track of 27 miles to Achill Sound, with a further 10 miles beyond that. No sooner was the railway open, than Mr J.R. Sheridan, the hotel proprietor, added 30 new rooms to his hotel. He asked the railway company for a grant of £20 with which he would buy another long car to operate from Achill station, where it would meet trains, to Dugort. This was agreed by the MGWR, and Sheridan began to operate a timetabled public service in the summer season of 1896. The details were:

	4-wheel long car with '2 or more horses'	2-wheel horse -drawn car		4-wheel long car with '2 or more horses'	2-wheel horse -drawn car
Dugort	11.10 am	2.30 pm	Achill Sta.	11.15 am	5.25 pm
Achill Sta.	12.50 pm	4.00 pm	Dugort	12.45 pm	7.05 pm

This was apparently a great success. The fare was 2s. 6d., including luggage. The MGWR told Sheridan that they were not to be held liable for anyone who 'hitched a lift'. By 1898, Sheridan asked for, and received, £50 per season for the service. A year later, the company was obliged to provide insurance cover for this service, and they told Sheridan that they were unhappy with the reliability of his horse-drawn conveyances. Correspondence between the company and the local authorities at the time indicate that the delays which were affecting Sheridan's reliability were in fact due to the very poor condition of the roads on Achill Island, all of which were little better than unsurfaced tracks. The company planned to operate the long car service themselves, and rented a horse stable at Dugort for the purpose in 1900. That summer, a mishap occurred - the car struck the bridge at Achill Sound and threw off some of its passengers. Matters must have improved after this, as in 1901 three services each way per day were offered, costing the company £326 for the season.

By this stage, long cars were becoming rarer in Ireland. However, the service offered had settled down very satisfactorily, and as late as 1905 the MGWR renewed the contract for some further years. A Mr Wallis offered to operate local sightseeing trips from Mallaranny and he hired horses, presumably to the hotel staff, for this purpose.

This service survived to become what is believed to have been Ireland's last regularly operated long car service. In 1913, the cars were advertised for sale at Dugort. Petrol-engined transport had arrived.

Further south, tourists were coming in increasing numbers to the remote and scenic region of Connemara. The company had bought two petrol-engined buses to operate a service from Clifden to Westport, and from time to time these were operated direct to the hotel at Mallaranny. At first these had solid rubber tyres, which must have resulted in a very uncomfortable ride on the stony roads of Connemara and Mayo. In 1924, the company's Engineer reported that 'giant pneumatic tyres' had been ordered for these buses.

Following decisions made in the early 1930s, the railway was originally due to close in 1934. Plans were made to introduce lorries to carry the line's goods traffic, and buses for the passengers. As noted previously, arrangements were made to stable a bus in the locomotive shed at Achill, and one of the two tracks into the shed was lifted to allow access. In addition, a bus garage was built in Westport, at a cost of £1,160. One 20-seater bus and one lorry were ordered, costing £4,560 altogether. However, it was recognised that at peak times this would be insufficient to meet the transport needs of the area. On the occasion of cattle fairs, lorries would have to be brought in from other areas, while four extra buses from Ballina depot would be needed to cope with the annual exodus of migratory farm workers. The GSR drew up a plan for a 4 ton cattle lorry in 1933, four of which were to be built.

A financial comparison between rail and road services, dated November 1933, showed that if the line was closed, the cost of dismantling it, plus the cost of establishing road services, would be more than paid for by the sale of scrap railway materials. In addition, the cost of upgrading the line for continued use would pay all the operating costs for road services for almost eight years. The result of this would be that all income from road services for this period would be extra, and in the long term would (hopefully) exceed the cost of providing the service.

It was noted that an Irish Omnibus Company vehicle was already carrying passengers on the route, and the GSR introduced a bus timetable which was similar to the train timetable, although the bus took 1½ hours to travel from Westport to Achill. Departures from Achill were at 11.00 am and 3.30 pm, while corresponding departures from Westport station were 1.15 pm and 8.30 pm. This enabled one bus, stabled at Achill, to work the entire service. In addition, on Newport Market Days the bus arriving at Westport at 12.30 (11.00 ex-Achill) had time to make an extra return trip to Newport before the afternoon service back to Achill. The Irish Omnibus Company's service of one bus per day between Ballina and Keel, on Achill Island, also served Mallaranny village. It was considered that hotel guests at Mallaranny would be adequately catered for by this service, as the buses connected with the trains at Westport - of 250 guests in July 1933, only 30 had travelled by train to Mallaranny.

At this stage, a report was prepared by the County Council outlining the state of the road to Achill. It was reported that

> ... the roadway between Westport and Newport is partly constructed of water-bound macadam and partly of tar macadam and is in reasonable condition. Between Newport and Mallaranny the surface of water-bound macadam is rough and potholed. The section between Mallaranny and Achill is also water-bound macadam, the width is narrow for bus and lorry traffic and the surface is very rough and potholed'.

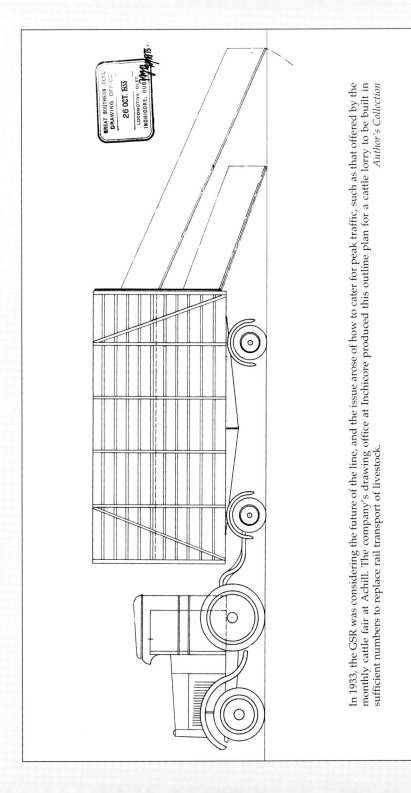

In 1933, the GSR was considering the future of the line, and the issue arose of how to cater for peak traffic, such as that offered by the monthly cattle fair at Achill. The company's drawing office at Inchicore produced this outline plan for a cattle lorry to be built in sufficient numbers to replace rail transport of livestock.

Author's Collection

Phone: **43147 & 8**
Wires: "Buses, Dublin,"

GREAT SOUTHERN RAILWAYS.

R. D. GRIFFITH,
Manager.

OMNIBUS DEPARTMENT.

D'OLIER HOUSE, D'OLIER STREET.

Your Ref. E.11042/5

DUBLIN,

Our Ref. 185

23rd June, 1934.

W.H.Morton Esq.,
General Manager,
Great Southern Railways,
KINGSBRIDGE.

Dear Sir,

CLOSING OF UNREMUNERATIVE BRANCH LINES.

I am in receipt of your letter of the 21st inst.
enclosing copy of letter received from Mr. Doyle,
Hotels Department.

The time-table proposed for the new Service
between Westport and Achill is as follows:-

Achill	dep	11.0 a.m.	3.45 p.m.
Westport	arr	12.30 p.m.	5.15 p.m.
Westport	dep	1.15 p.m.	8.30 p.m.
Achill	arr	2.45 p.m.	10.0 p.m.

In addition, the Ballina/Keel Service passes
through Mallaranny on weekdays, leaving Mallaranny each
morning at 9.10 a.m. and returning from Ballina at 4.30
p.m. each evening.

Yours faithfully,

R. D. Griffith
Per

LM/VR.

Great Southern Railways—Omnibus Department

ON AND AFTER

Monday, 31st December, 1934

The following Services will operate between

Achill and Westport

ON WEEK-DAYS ONLY

			A.M.	A.M.	P.M.
ACHILL	..	.. dep.	8.33	11. 0	3.45
MALLARANNY	..	„	9.10	11.37	4.22
NEWPORT	..	„	9.45	12.12	4.57
WESTPORT	..	arr.	10.10	12.37	5.22
			P.M.	P.M.	P.M.
WESTPORT	..	dep.	1.15	6.30	8.30
NEWPORT	..	„	1.40	6.55	8.55
MALLARANNY	..	„	2.15	7.30	9.30
ACHILL	..	.. arr.	2.50	8. 5	10. 5

D'OLIER HOUSE,
　D'OLIER STREET,
　　DUBLIN, C. 5.
'PHONES 48147/8.

W. H. MORTON,
　　General Manager.
14th December. 1934.

Poster produced to advertise the bus service introduced after the passenger train was withdrawn in 1934. However, the roads were unfit for buses, and after four months the passenger service was restored until road improvements were carried out. *Author's Collection*

The County Surveyor therefore concluded in November 1933 that while a 32-seater bus would be permissible, lorries of over two tons weight could not be allowed beyond Mallaranny. Following an appeal by the company, it was reluctantly conceded that a three-axle lorry of four tons could be allowed, as the weight would be spread over an extra axle. The GSR made it clear that they wanted the County Council to upgrade the road as soon as possible.

As has been seen, the state of the road was the sole reason that the line did not close entirely in 1934. The passenger service was to be operated by buses, but the line was to remain open for goods traffic until the road was improved. From 31st December 1934, the bus service was as shown opposite.

Owing to the delay in upgrading the road, a passenger service was re-introduced again in April 1935. When the line finally closed completely on 30th September, 1937, a service of three buses per day commenced. Buses left Achill at 8.50, 11.10 am and 3.30 pm. In the other direction, departures from Westport were at 1.25, 6.15 and 8.30 pm. With minor modifications, this was to remain the pattern for many years afterwards, though a 1947 timetable shows the third service operating on Achill Fair Day only. By this stage, Achill station was no longer the terminus - buses ran onto the island and terminated at Dooagh.

Great Southern Railways bus at Leenane, Co. Galway, 1934. This bus was used on the Clifden-Westport-Mallaranny Hotel route operated for tourists by the railway. Buses of this type were used to operate the early bus services which replaced the railway to Achill.

H.C. Casserley, courtesy R. Casserley

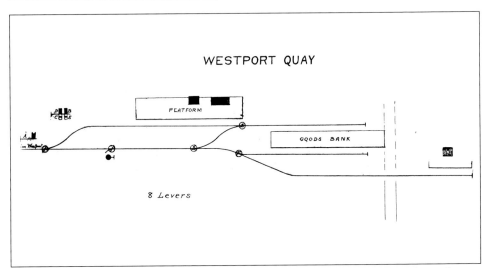

Track plan and signalling installations, Westport Quay. Photographic evidence shows that further tracks were added at a later stage. *Author's Collection*

Gradient profile of Westport Quay Line. *H.C.A. Beaumont Collection*

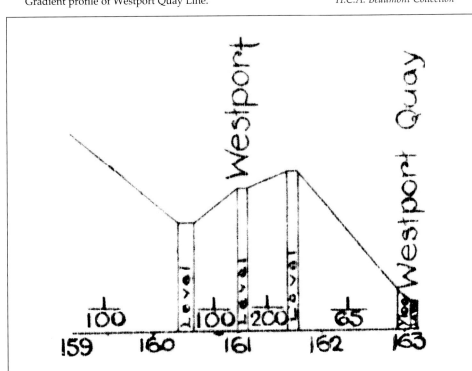

Chapter Thirteen

The Westport Quay Line

Mention has already been made of the Westport Quay line. While this was not actually part of the Achill branch, its story is related. Much of the goods traffic from the Achill line was for Westport Quay, and would have been transferred to the Quay line once it arrived in Westport. In addition, for the first few years of the Achill line's life, passengers were able to travel down to the Quay.

In 1866, the Great Northern and Western Railway (GNWR) had opened its line to Westport Town station. From the outset, it was worked by the Midland Great Western, and later absorbed into it. Westport was a port of some importance at that time, and a railway connection with the Quay had been planned since the railway had come to Westport. However, due to financial disagreements between the GNWR and the MGWR, while construction of the Quay line was undertaken in the mid-1860s, it was not until 1874 that it was opened to traffic. Even then, it was 'third time lucky', as the line had failed two Board of Trade inspections within the year prior to opening. The line was just under two miles long, and immediately proved useful for the carriage of goods to and from the Quay, but the Harbour Commissioners also requested that the company operate passenger trains during the 'bathing season'. The MGWR refused at first, but finally agreed in 1880 to operate a seasonal service. This must have been successful, as the passenger service was later extended to operate all year round. However, by 1889 it had again become a summer-only service. Further requests to the company in 1892 to re-instate the winter service were turned down. Even the summer service ended as early as 1st November, 1901, after which the line remained open for goods traffic only. The service provided in 1897, and which was probably typical, was as follows:

		Weekdays only					Weekdays only		
		Pass.	Mixed	Pass.			Pass.	Mixed	Goods
		am	pm	pm			am	am	pm
Westport	dep.	9.38	3.00*	4.00	Westport Quay	dep.	7.50	10.00	3.30*
Westport Quay	arr.	9.43	3.15	4.05	Westport	arr.	7.55	10.05	3.50

* A footnote in the Working Timetable stated that these trains could make a second trip when necessary.

It will be noted that there were two passenger-carrying trains in the uphill direction, and three in the down direction. Doubtless, a passenger brake vehicle was used on the 3.30 return as the brake vehicle for this goods working. Passenger trains were allowed five minutes for the journey in either direction, while goods or mixed trains were allowed 15 minutes in the downhill direction, and a very generous 20 minutes in the uphill direction.

In January 1895, the station master at the Quay station absconded with the takings from the station. This sort of occurrence was not unknown in other districts as well, and was occasionally a result of the former employee wishing to emigrate to start a new and more prosperous life elsewhere!

Westport Quay, approximately 1895. Goods wagons line each side of the quay platform, the two on the right being full of bags of grain.   *Lawrence Collection, courtesy National Library of Ireland*

Looking towards Westport Quay, with Croagh Patrick mountain in the distance, 1967.
J.P. O'Dea Collection, courtesy National Library of Ireland

After 1901, the line existed for goods traffic only. One or two return trains per day were timetabled, but in later years goods trains only operated when required. The service in 1930 was as follows, and again a footnote mentioned that repeat trips could be operated if necessary to clear traffic:

Weekdays only - Goods only

		am	pm			am	pm
Westport	*dep.*	9.40	1.50	Westport Quay *dep.*		10.20	2.30
Westport Quay *arr.*		9.55	2.05	Westport	*arr.*	10.40	2.50

From 27th July, 1931, signalling equipment was decommissioned and the line was worked under the 'one engine in steam' regulations. In July 1969, the track across the road from the Quay station and onto the Quay was lifted, having seen very little use for some time. By the 1970s the traffic on offer had become a mere trickle, and the line was kept in order to allow CIE to haul tank wagons of diesel fuel down to their bus garage, now situated beside the old station. Visits to Westport Quay around this period revealed a line that seemed asleep rather than derelict. A rusty water column was still in place beside the track which had crossed the road onto the Quay itself, but the track across the road had been removed some years earlier. The old passenger platform and the long disused building on it were still extant and in good condition, while the goods platform was overgrown, but had a siding adjacent to it. A run-round loop was still in place.

By 1978, no train had traversed the line for some time, and the track had been partly lifted. The line was to all intents and purposes abandoned. In the early 1980s, all but about half a mile of track was taken up, and the line was closed. The remaining short section lingered on as a siding and was used to load timber trains leaving Westport until 2001.

A rare passenger working on the Westport Quay line. In June 1964, some 18 months after the end of steam traction on CIE, an extensive steam-hauled tour of Ireland was organised by the Irish Railway Record Society and the Railway Correspondence & Travel Society. This trip, over a number of days, attracted a large number of enthusiasts from all over Ireland and the UK. On 10th June, the train reached Westport Quay station.

H.C. Casserley, courtesy R. Casserley

Westport Quay station - a rare view from the road side before the station building was demolished. The picture was taken on the occasion of the IRRS/RCTS tour of 1964.

H.C. Casserley, courtesy R. Casserley

The IRRS/RCTS railtour on 10th June, 1964 is seen here on its return from Westport Quay as it climbs towards Westport Town station. The locomotive was a former Great Southern & Western 0-6-0 and the coaches a mix of 1950s CIE-built stock and ex-GSWR stock. By this stage, few if any passenger vehicles of Midland Great Western origin survived in use.

H.C. Casserley, courtesy R. Casserley

Classic view of the Westport Quay line, taken in 1975. 'A' class No. 001 climbs up the Quay line towards Westport Town station with light load. In the background the holy mountain, Croagh Patrick, looms. A glimpse of what the Achill line itself would have looked like had it survived into diesel days.   *Barry Carse*

'A' class diesel locomotive No. 001 shunts wagons at Westport Quay, Saturday 15th March, 1975. These locomotives were the most numerous class of diesel to operate in Ireland (so far). Sixty of them were delivered in 1955, and three managed to make it to their 40th year in traffic in 1995.   *Barry Carse*

The Westport Quay line was short but steeply graded. After a brief and slight uphill gradient after leaving the Town station, the line descended to the sea at a ruling gradient of 1 in 65. This necessitated special arrangements to prevent trains losing control as they negotiated this descent. A brake van had to be provided at each end of the train, and no more than 10 wagons were permitted. At the Quay, there was a short passenger platform on the down side, with a run-round loop. Beyond this, a goods platform provided modest loading and unloading facilities, with a crane being provided. The line continued across the road to the actual quays themselves where there were a number of privately owned sidings. Hall's Mill had a short tramway which connected with the railway, and there were special instructions for wagons worked onto the tramway. These quayside tramways fell into disuse about 1930. A brake van was to be kept at the Quay, to which all wagons were to be coupled, and locomotives were prohibited - presumably Hall's had horses to pull wagons. Messrs Maude and Sons also had a siding there, and the instructions here were that all wagons worked onto their tracks must be attached to an engine at all times. This appears to have been due to a gradient on this siding. There was a water crane at Westport Quay station, so that a locomotive could take on water here without having to go back up to the Town station. However, no turntable was provided here, so that locomotives working the line had to travel tender-first in one direction.

Today, no trace remains of Westport Quay station. The site has been swept away and re-developed as holiday accommodation. Part of the short route up to the Town station remains as a footpath.

The Westport Quay line survives in part. About a quarter of the track was used as a siding for storage of timber wagons until 2001. This siding ends at the 162nd milepost, visible at the right of the buffer stop. The track was completely relaid in 2000, as can be seen in this photograph taken at Easter 2001. Behind the photographer, nature has reclaimed the line.
Author

Chapter Fourteen

Recollections and Anecdotes

Like any railway line, the Achill line had its fair share of stories to be told. The line served an area that was then very much less developed than it is today, though it could be very busy at times.

At the time that research was in progress for this book, it was some 60 years since the Achill line had closed, and it was difficult to meet many people who had personal memories of it. However, we are fortunate in being able to share a few recollections, which the author collected from a small number of people who remembered the line.

Fair days at Achill brought a large number of people into the area once a month, and there would be busy scenes at Achill station where cattle were loaded for export. The several bars at Achill Sound would do a roaring trade, although this was not without its problems - one at least used to close early on fair days to discourage over indulgence!

A tradition among railwaymen in past years was that there was at one time a poitin* still at the back of the locomotive shed at Achill station. It was claimed that this had been put together using parts taken from locomotives, in particular injector pipes. Whatever the origin of the still, the story continues that eventually management in Dublin *did* hear about it, and closed the locomen's dormitory as a result. In the line's later years, while there was a locomotive based at Achill, the dorm could conceivably have been dispensed with. The only details of locomen's lodging turns which have survived include the reminiscences of one driver who used to claim that the overnight stay in Achill was a favourite of the enginemen, because there was 'a drop of holy water' (= poitin) available after the long journey to Achill, along with a game of cards with the station master. One locomotive cleaner, Patrick Ginnety, employed at Achill, was reprimanded in 1901 because he had let a man (presumably not a railway employee) sleep in the locomotive shed. Could this have been related to the poitin story? In the 1920s a still was indeed seized by the Revenue Authorities at Achill station, and a railwayman was apprehended. The distilling apparatus was of such sophisticated construction that it was removed to Dublin for preservation. The railwayman concerned had other hidden talents - it was also discovered that he was an accomplished manufacturer of counterfeit coins!

One employee on the Achill line at one time asked for a transfer to another part of the country, as he wanted to distance himself from a young lady in the locality - we can only wonder why! After his transfer, he arranged for a local newspaper to publish an obituary notice about him so that he would not be traced. In the 1920s and 1930s the line's locomotive foreman, John Brown of Westport, would appear at Achill station on a motorbike driven by one of his staff. He would return in the cab of the locomotive, having encouraged his assistant to race the train back to Westport!

As well as fair day cattle traffic, the railway carried considerable quantities of fish and eggs from Achill, which were sent by the afternoon train to Dublin for

---

* Poitin (pronounced 'potcheen') was an illegally distilled spirit traditionally made from potatoes.

sale in the markets there the next day. The fish siding at Tonregee has already been referred to - having only been in use for a few years the whole catch was subsequently loaded at Achill. No former employees or indeed local people who survived into the period in which this account was written have any recollection of this siding, and indeed one expressed doubt whether it had ever existed - thus emphasising how little it had been used. However, in the line's later days, trains would stop here on request for passengers or mail to be offloaded.

Harvest workers were the line's third source of short-lived bustle. As already mentioned, large numbers of teenagers and young adults used to leave the area to travel to Britain for seasonal farm work, returning home with a much appreciated pay packet some months later. Special trains often had to be laid on to transport them, and as many as 250 people would leave in a single day. For example, between 18th March and 1st July, 1933, 1,357 people left Achill, with another 67 from Mallaranny and 30 from Newport. On three days within this period special trains were operated from Achill at 9.00 am, to connect with a train which left Westport at 10.30 for Dublin. On another three days, special trains left Achill at 6.00 am, to connect with the 8.00 train at Westport. The largest number that travelled on one of these specials was 251, on 13th June - this would have been enough people to almost fill a five-coach train. On the other days that specials operated, they carried numbers between 123 and 177, though on one day only there were a mere 29. It would seem that a special train for these passengers was somewhat extravagant, but a feature of this traffic was the considerable amount of luggage that accompanied the passengers, and in addition to the carriages, several goods vans had to be added to the train to accommodate it all. The steamer to Scotland left Dublin at 6.30 in the evening.

The recollections of two locomotive firemen included their mention of how the wind would suddenly become noticeable after they left Mallaranny, heading downhill towards Owenduff. One man was taken by surprise - having tended the fire, he was leaning over the cab side enjoying the scenery as the locomotive coasted downhill, when the wind whipped his cap off his head and tossed it into the ferns at the side of the line - where it remained! Another former fireman told of his first and only trip over the line, which was shortly before it closed. It was dark when he travelled over the line, and he did not know the area. His driver warned him of the tunnels approaching Newport, referring to them as the 'Black Holes'. On reaching Mallaranny, the wind became noticeable around the hill above the Belmullet Road, and he could smell the sea air for the first time, mixed with the coal smoke and hot oil of the engine. Achill locomotive shed was seen as a remote outpost, with little in the way of comfort for an engineman after a long journey. Locomotive crews would work into Achill principally from Athlone, lodge overnight, and return with the first train the next day. However there was one locomotive driver based at Achill throughout most of the line's life, and possibly more in the earlier days. A steam raiser was also stationed at Achill. Neither Mallaranny nor Newport had locomotive sheds, so no crews were based there.

Mallaranny had the hotel, of course. When it was first opened, the company widely advertised the beneficial nature of the fresh air and local climate. Perhaps at the request of the hotel management, Mallaranny's station master began to record the daily temperature, sunshine and rainfall; and his successors carried the tradition on. The last station master carried on recording this information for years after the line closed - right until his death in 1956, in fact.

An elderly lady at Achill used to recall the line in the 1910s. At the time she lived at Tonregee and as a child would wait to see the train pass in the evenings. She recalled three porters who stayed at a relative's house, who worked in Achill station. They were natives of Connemara. In 1921, a Mr Considine came as station master to Achill, replacing a Mr Coughlan. He was originally from County Donegal, and when the line closed in 1937 he was transferred to Athboy, Co. Meath. A depot keeper was appointed in his place as an agent for lorry traffic, and he took up residence in the station house for a while until it was sold off. His name was Long, and he was originally from Co. Cork, having been transferred when the old Cork & Macroom line had been closed. These memories bear out the fact that railway staff in those days were likely to be transferred to wherever the company saw fit to station them.

In the 1920s, an Englishman named T.R. Perkins set himself the task of travelling over every railway line throughout the British Isles. His written accounts of this adventurous undertaking included the Achill line, which he reached in 1934. Perkins wrote of travelling by train to Clifden, and continuing onwards to Westport via the company's tourist bus. By this stage, tourist buses would continue to Mallaranny, rather than deposit passengers at Westport station. We take up Perkins' story as he arrived at the Hotel.

> I continued in the bus to Mallaranny and had tea in the Railway Company's fine hotel, afterwards exploring the beautifully laid out grounds, from which a glorious panorama over Clew Bay - with its many islands - is unfolded. On the northern side the head of one of the creeks of Blacksod Bay comes very near to the hotel and the view in this direction is equally fine, though of a different character. As at Recess the climate at Mallaranny encourages the growth of palms and other exotic plants, the situations being remarkably sheltered.
>
> [On his return journey the following day, he commented:] Mallaranny is two hundred feet higher than Achill - so that our rate - with a good load of wagons - was a crawl up the 1 in 70 gradients. We arrived at Mallaranny and spent an infinity shunting, as well as taking on quite a surprising load of passengers, some being young fellows off to work on English farms for the summer.
>
> Onward to Westport I discovered the views from the train were far superior to those obtained on the road on the Saturday evening - the railway runs high on the hillside, the wide expanse of island studded Clew Bay stretching below us for miles, while the great cone of Croagh Patrick dominated the horizon beyond. Fuchsias abound at Mallaranny and the heather must be a glorious sight when it comes into bloom.

The scenery along the line was commented on frequently. Between Achill and Mallaranny the country was totally unspoilt, and the fact that the railway line was closer to the coast than the road added to the scenic value of a journey. Between Mallaranny and Newport the line travelled high up on the hillside, again allowing spectacular views not seen from the road. In Newport, there was the viaduct, followed by two tunnels on the way to Westport. The stretch between here and Westport travelled through totally different scenery, with farmland and drumlin style hills being more prominent. For today's traveller, the railway may be gone, but the scenery is still there to be enjoyed.

Mallaranny station 15 years after closure. The trackbed is overgrown, the passenger shelter on the up platform is boarded up, and the signal box has been demolished. Apart from that, little has changed. The goods shed in the distance later became a church hall, while the main station building on the extreme right was to remain structurally sound for another half-century after the photograph was taken. The water tower still stands. *Irish Railway Record Society*

Westport, 10th June 1964. Straight ahead, a locomotive is parked on the line which continues on to Westport Quay, while the long siding formed by the remaining first half-mile or so of the Achill line curves away to the right, past the goods shed. On the left, in front of the engine shed is ex-Great Southern & Western 'J15' class 0-6-0 No. 186. Locomotives of this type were rare visitors to Westport even after the amalgamation, although they were by far the most numerous class of engine in Ireland, and were widely travelled elsewhere. On this occasion, No. 186 was participating in the forerunner of the Railway Preservation Society of Ireland's (RPSI) famous May weekend railtours - an all-Ireland steam tour organised by the IRRS and RCTS. Shortly afterwards, No. 186 was presented to the RPSI by CIE, and became one of only 16 or so Irish broad gauge steam engines to have survived in preservation. The RPSI owns or operates nine of these, and happily 186 is one. She survived to become arguably the most widely travelled Irish steam engine of all, covering every remaining line in the country since preservation. The RPSI used her until 1981, when she went into retirement awaiting future overhaul. At the time of writing (early 2002) she was under major repair in the RPSI's workshop in County Antrim.

H.C. Casserley, courtesy R. Casserley

Chapter Fifteen

After Closure

Following closure, the preparations for final abandonment of the line continued apace. Remaining coal stocks at Achill were removed, and the contents of the station buildings were taken away. On 1st October, 1937, a special train operated over the line to collect empty wagons left at the three stations. This journey was not without incident: the train ran over a sheep on the way, and the owner submitted an insurance claim against the GSR! By this stage the line was in a very run-down state, with paint fading and peeling on buildings and signals, and fencing and track in poor repair. Doubtless the unfortunate sheep would have had no difficulty in finding its way onto the line.

The following day, locomotive No. 530 made a final journey to Achill to collect a further half-dozen goods wagons that had been left in the final few days for unloading. A small group posed for a photograph with the locomotive crew, and watched as the short train left in the afternoon sun. The line now slumbered, though Achill station was to continue as a road goods depot, and the bus was using the locomotive shed as a garage. Road freight depot managers were appointed to Newport and Achill, and the former station master at Achill, Mr Considine, was transferred to Athboy, Co. Meath, for the remainder of his career.

Altogether, 30 jobs were lost on the line. The staffing structure was:

Three	Station masters
Four	Signal porters
One	Goods checker
One	General porter (Achill)
Six	Gangers
Twelve	Platelayers (track maintenance staff)
One	Steam raiser (Achill)
One	Locomotive fireman (Achill)
One	Locomotive driver (Achill)

All clerical staff were absorbed into other jobs on the railway with the exception of the Newport station master, who was pensioned off. The track maintenance men were not so fortunate - those with short service, or temporarily employed, became redundant. Unless they had reached 65 years of age, no pension was paid to them. The three locomotive crewmen based at Achill were pensioned off, at an annual cost of £310 for all three!

The GSR had been in correspondence with the rating authorities regarding the issue of paying rates on abandoned railway lines. The GSR protested that a reduction should be made, as the redundant premises were no longer being used to gather income, but the Government insisted that this could only be arranged if the track was lifted. As a result, plans were made to remove all the track without delay.

The task of disposal of other assets now started. Almost immediately some land was sold to Mayo County Council. Part of the road improvements took the

Diesel power on the Achill line. The first half mile of the Achill line remained as a siding out of Westport station until the early 1980s. Here, a General Motors '071' class locomotive, built almost 40 years after the line closed, shunts wagons on this remaining short spur of the line; 17th April, 1981.   *Barry Carse*

General Motors '121' class diesel locomotive No. B127 turns at Westport station after arriving with a train of mail vans from Dublin, early 1970s.   *Barry Carse*

form of re-routing a short section of the main road over the line at Furnace Lough, Burrishoole, between Newport and Mallaranny. The railway bridge over the Lough inlet was demolished, and a new road bridge built using the bases of the original piers. Between Newport and Westport, several other short stretches of line were also used to facilitate road improvements. Sweeney's of Achill Sound rented some accommodation at the old station there for a time. The railway lay in limbo over the winter, and in January 1938 the GSR accepted a tender for £6,550 from the Hammond Lane Foundry Co. in Dublin to lift the track and remove other steelwork. By mid-1938, the rails had all gone, save for a half-mile stretch outside Westport station, which was to remain for many years longer as a siding. However, all of the station buildings and the water towers at Achill and Mallaranny were left behind, and still stand today having now witnessed more silence during their lives than working use. The stations and land were sold by various lots over subsequent years. As late as 1945, Loughan Lake and water supply at Achill were sold to the County Council, along with Achill station (now no longer used as a bus and lorry depot) and part of the track bed near Burrishoole.

Only the hotel had a future with the Great Southern Railways. Despite it being nearly 20 miles from what was now the nearest railhead at Westport, the GSR retained it as part of its Great Southern Hotels Group. When the GSR was absorbed into Coras Iompair Eireann in 1945, and CIE itself was nationalised in 1950, the hotel found itself as part of a nationalised transport concern, through CIE's hotel operating subsidiary, OIE. The old station at Mallaranny was still part of this property, along with a mile of track bed either side of it. It was not until 1977 that CIE sold the hotel to private owners, but changing tourism patterns had made it something of an anachronism by then and it was clear after several periods of closure and re-opening in the 1980s that in its existing form it could not survive. By 1991 after unsuccessful efforts to rescue it by a local consortium, it had closed its doors as a traditional hotel for the last time.

The life of the railway to Achill spanned some 42 years before the tracks were taken up in 1938. However, a little known survivor was the first half-mile or so of the line which remained *in situ* as a siding out of Westport station for the same length of time after the rest of the line was lifted. This view dates from August 1978. A few years later, this last stretch of the rails to Achill was also removed.   *Author*

Newport station exterior. Similar in style to Westport, but smaller. This picture shows the station building in 2001, from the road side. The railway tracks were immediately on the other side of the building.   *Author*

Locomotive water tower and coaling stage at Achill, well preserved in 2001. Many remnants of the line have survived, now having witnessed many more years of disuse than the activity they were built for.   *Author*

Westport station, 2001. *Upper*: the up platform, now the terminus of trains from Dublin. The Westport Quay and Achill lines continued beyond this platform. *Lower*: On the down platform, this attractive waiting shelter remains. Little use is made of this side of the station nowadays.

(Both) Author

Bridge over railway line near Owengarve River, 2000. The stone ballast which carried the track is still visible on the surface, almost 70 years since the last train ran.   *Catherine Beaumont*

The bridge which carried the line out of Westport remains over Altamont Street, the town's station being at the top of the hill just beyond it. The reason for the bridge's survival was that the first half-mile or so remained as a siding out of Westport station until the late 1970s/early 1980s. It was at this point that one of the railway's few accidents occurred: in June 1896 a runaway wagon careered over the edge, landing on the roof of a house below the line. Fortunately, and miraculously, nobody was injured.   *Author*

Like the hotel, much of the route of the line remains. Until the early 1970s it was possible to walk almost the entire route of the line, save for the section at Burrishoole where the road had been diverted onto the old trackbed to improve its course after the track was lifted. At Westport, the station is now the terminus of the train service from Dublin, though it now handles passenger traffic only, the goods trains having been withdrawn during the 1980s. The first half-mile or so of the track to Achill remained *in situ* until the 1980s as a siding out of Westport station, the long viaduct being retained to carry it. Between Westport and Newport much of the line may still be traced, including the two tunnels outside Newport. In Newport, the viaduct over the river has been beautifully restored and forms an attractive centrepiece in the town, especially when floodlit at night. The station there spent some time as a Garda (Police) station but is now a private residence, while the goods shed has been converted into a small Chapel. Building work has since covered the course of the line particularly on the Achill side of the station, and there is no longer any trace of the old goods yard and cattle bank there, this area having been redeveloped in the 1970s. The route remains undisturbed from outside Newport the whole way to Mallaranny (now usually called Mulrany), where the station is derelict, having remained as an outbuilding to the hotel (a case of the tail wagging the dog!) until about 1991. The platforms and water tower are intact, and the goods shed is a Church hall. The route of the line continues across the Belmullet Road, and becomes overgrown over the next few miles, but otherwise undisturbed. Nearer to Achill, locals have utilised some of the old formation as access roads to fields and private houses. Achill station has had a variety of uses since the GSR's buses left it in the 1940s, but it is now a Bed & Breakfast, and the goods shed and locomotive shed, while standing, are derelict. Mr Hector's Fish Store has outlived the lot - while Hector's operation is long gone, Bord Iascaigh Mara (Irish Fishery Board) occupy the building today. Along the line, original boundaries may be seen in various places. The stone walls remain on each side of the line for much of its route several miles either side of Mallaranny, and elsewhere lineside fencing still contains an occasional sleeper. At the turn of the 21st century, there were one or two locations where original half-round sleepers were to be seen - these would have been part of a fencing boundary for almost a century.

In the late 1990s, there was a plan to develop several miles of the trackbed near Mulrany as a working railway museum. A carriage of the type used on the line and a small steam locomotive were to be brought to the site and used to operate a short train ride for tourists. Unfortunately, this plan did not proceed. While preserved steam railway operations are very popular tourist attractions elsewhere, the costs of operating and maintaining a steam locomotive are very high, and only a location with a very large number of potential passengers is suitable for the establishment of such an attraction. That said, it is tempting to speculate that with the continuing development of tourism in the area, perhaps some day a railway-based attraction of some sort may prove feasible.

The area the railway served now has a road system that would have been unimaginable in 1895, and public transport is provided by a fast service of modern buses operated by Bus Eireann, the road passenger subsidiary of CIE. Still, even without the Achill line, this area is well worth a visit for the friendly people, good food and spectacular scenery.

Appendix One

Working the Railway

The following are extracts from working timetables and special instructions issued to staff, with particular reference to the Achill line.

Tickets

Market traders could be issued with tickets at cheap rates as follows:
Tuesdays: Mallaranny to Newport.
Thursdays: Achill, Mallaranny or Newport to Westport.

Tickets on all trains were checked at Newport. This recalls the fact that most trains on the line did not have through corridors, so that an on-train ticket checker could not have moved down the train as it travelled.

The fares in 1927 between Dublin and the two intermediate stations on the line were as follows:

Limited Mail Fares	Single						Return					
	First			Third			First			Third		
	£	s.	d.	£	s.	d.	£	s.	d.	£	s.	d.
Newport	2	9	0	1	7	7	4	5	11	2	15	2
Mallaranny	2	11	8	1	9	6	4	10	5	2	18	0

Ordinary Fares	Single						Return					
	First			Third			First			Third		
	£	s.	d.	£	s.	d.	£	s.	d.	£	s.	d.
Newport	2	3	2	1	4	8	3	16	5	2	9	4
Mallaranny	2	5	10	1	6	1	4	0	11	2	12	2

Weekend Fares	First			Third		
	£	s.	d.	£	s.	d..
Newport	2	17	7	1	12	10
Mallaranny	3	1	1	1	14	10

The fares are quoted in pounds, shillings and pence, the currency of the time. At the time, a railway porter earned about £100 per year, so a train fare of, say, £3, represented 3 per cent of his annual wage, or a week and a half's pay. Small wonder that many people did not travel to the extent that they do nowadays!

Surviving traffic figures show that Westport-bound passenger trains tended to pick up most of their passengers at Newport. All tickets were therefore inspected at Newport on trains in this direction.

A first class return ticket for tourist traffic between Dublin and Mallaranny, for the railway company's hotel, c.1900.

Ernie Shepherd

Live stock trains

Trains carrying cattle were to be given precedence over all other trains except passenger trains. Instructions were issued in 1920 that their progress was to be telegraphed or telephoned to the next station along the line to ensure that no delays took place. Timings were set down as follows:

Section	Load not exceeding 30 Wagons Minutes	Loads exceeding 30 Wagons Minutes
Achill to Mallaranny	20	25
Mallaranny to Newport	25	31
Newport to Westport	19	24

The maximum amount of wagons allowed on a cattle train over the Achill line was 34 loaded wagons, however only 30 vehicles were allowed on a train of empty wagons.

On all trains between Mallaranny and Achill, the guard had to be ready to pin down brakes when descending the long stretch of 1 in 70 west of Mallaranny.

Signalling

After the passage of the last train each night, the lights on the signals (oil lamps) had to be extinguished. In the morning they were to be lit again. In the case of Mallaranny station, this meant quite a walk for the unfortunate employee entrusted with the task, as the distant signal in the up direction was a mile beyond Mallaranny station, and on an exposed stretch of the line! The only exception to this rule was when a special train operating during the night - but such instances on the Achill line were very few and far between. In frosty or snowy weather, signals and points were to be periodically tested all night in case they froze in one position.

Trains approaching stations, or involved in shunting manoeuvres had whistling codes to assist signalmen. At Westport, the following were used:

Train from Westport Quay:	2 long whistles.
From Achill line:	3 long whistles.

Crane Power at stations, and accommodation for dealing with traffic

For loading and unloading goods from trains, each goods platform was provided with a small crane. At Achill, Mallaranny, and Westport these were of 1½ ton capacity, while that at Newport could handle 2 tons. By comparison, the crane on Westport Quay was of 5 ton capacity, to assist in unloading boats.

Each station on the line was equipped with a 'Carriage Dock' or ramp at the end of one of the goods sidings where road carts or vehicles could be loaded on and off wagons.

A 20 ton rail-borne steam crane was kept at Athlone for use on a number of western lines, including Achill, in case of breakdowns or emergencies. In Great Southern days, the maintenance of the track was managed from Limerick.

Composition of trains

Only four-coupled locomotives were allowed over the line, due to the light track and severity of some curves. The only known exception to this is the 'E' class 0-6-0 tank engines which were used on the line when it opened, but were banned by 1920. In later years, 'G2' class 2-4-0s made occasional appearances, but 'D16' 4-4-0s and ex-GSWR 'D17' 4-4-0s covered all day-to-day traffic.

However, a 1920s Great Southern Appendix includes a table of engines grouped according to power and size, and lists the various engine classes allowed over certain routes. The entry for the Achill line has a number of locomotive classes shown, though it is doubtful whether many of these classes, especially the ex-GSWR tank engines, actually did ever travel as far as the Achill line. Those allowed were as follows:

GSR class	Type	Engine Group (see below)	Origin
D14	4-4-0	O	Great Southern & Western Railway
G3	2-4-0	O	Waterford, Limerick & Western Railway
D15	4-4-0	O	Waterford, Limerick & Western Railway
G2	2-4-0	O	Midland Great Western Railway
C4	4-4-2T	OT	Great Southern & Western Railway
C5	4-4-2T	OT	Waterford, Limerick & Western Railway
E1	0-4-4T	OT	Waterford, Limerick & Western Railway
E2	0-4-4T	PT	Waterford, Limerick & Western Railway
J26	0-6-0T	PT	Midland Great Western Railway
D19	4-4-0	R	Great Southern & Western Railway
D17	4-4-0	R	Great Southern & Western Railway
D16	4-4-0	R	Midland Great Western Railway
F6	2-4-2T	RT	Great Southern & Western Railway
C7	4-4-2T	RT	Great Southern & Western Railway

Engine group	Maximum No. of empty wagons
O	45
OT	40
PT	35
R	35
RT	30

It was recommended that passenger trains should have a brake vehicle at the back of the train in normal circumstances, i.e. no passenger carrying vehicles outside it. However, if absolutely necessary, up to four passenger carrying vehicles were allowed to trail behind it. A mixed train is to have the goods wagons behind the passenger vehicles, and no more than 30 vehicles of all descriptions were allowed.

'Distinctive Head-Lights' were to be carried by all engines, and were to be lit in foggy weather and after dark. The signalman at each station was able to identify the type of train approaching according to the lamps carried, according to a code:

Type of Train	Lamp code
All Passenger and Mixed Trains	Two white lights - one above each buffer
Goods and Cattle Trains	One white light above left buffer

A rail-borne inspection cycle was kept for use on line inspections. On various lines with severe gradients, sharp curves or tunnels, use of this was restricted or prohibited in case those pedalling it lost control. Its use was banned between Mallaranny and Achill, unless it was signalled as a train, i.e. unless the line was kept clear for it as if it were a train. However, no restrictions applied to its use in the tunnels at Newport.

Train movements and Shunting

Some interesting regulations governing shunting manoeuvres in Mallaranny station have survived. The station was fairly level, but either side of it was a long gradient, about a mile of 1 in 70 uphill towards Newport, and the same downhill towards Achill. The goods sidings faced Newport, therefore a train backing wagons into them would be moving in the direction of Achill as it entered them. Should a runaway occur before entering the sidings, it would have been propelled through the station and would have set off downhill, probably derailing on the reverse curves a mile or more down the line. As a result there were elaborate regulations in connection with wagon brakes being applied while shunting was in progress. If the locomotive left a line of wagons on the main line, at least six of them had to have their brakes pinned down, and sprags used under the wheels to eliminate the possibility of a runaway. The station master at Mallaranny had to ensure he always had a supply of wooden sprags! Another rule stated that any vehicle not fitted with a vacuum brake was to be pulled, rather than pushed, in a downhill direction. If a wagon was to be pulled into the Mallaranny sidings, the locomotive would not have been able to get out. It must be presumed that the very short stretch of level track adjacent to the sidings' entrance would have been used as an excuse to circumvent this. Similar warnings and arrangements applied to Westport station, as well as Westport Quay.

When ballast or other maintenance trains came to the line, the movement of men and materials back and forth might lead to a necessity to pull or push the train over short distances where work was in progress. Pushing of wagons was prohibited on gradients in the vicinity of Westport, Mallaranny and also just outside Achill station, for the same reasons as outlined above.

At Westport, a 44 ft 10 in. locomotive turntable was installed. At Achill, only an inspection pit was provided at the outset, the 'E' class tank engines working bunker first in one direction. However, very soon after the opening, a turntable the same size as that at Westport was added. Watering facilities were available at Achill, both at a 8,110 gallon water tower and inside the shed, though the supply in the shed had fallen into disuse by the mid-1920s. At Mallaranny, a water tower was situated at the Westport end of the up platform, and a water crane on the opposite end of the down platform, with a joint capacity of 8,840 gallons. Newport had a crane on the down platform with 4,750 gallons capacity.

Traffic Statistics Relating to Closure

Before the Achill line closed, much research was undertaken both by the GSR and by local business interests, into the traffic carried by the railway. The GSR hoped to make a case for closing it, while local interests wanted to be able to illustrate the benefit the line was to the community. Some official returns of goods tonnages and passenger numbers have survived and are worth analysing. The following figures all relate to the year 1930, upon which the Great Southern Railways based their studies and calculations on whether they felt the line was viable or not.

Westport and Achill Branch
Receipts and Expenditure 1930

RECEIPTS	Branch traffic			Between Achill line stations and stations beyond			Total	Contributory value of branch to rest of system		
	Summer	Winter	Total	Summer	Winter	Total	Total	Summer	Winter	Total
	£	£	£	£	£	£	£	£	£	£
Passengers	376	337	713	515	403	918	1,631	3,117	2,304	5,421
Season Tickets	-	-	-	2	21	23	23	30	316	346
Parcels etc.	21	22	43	129	90	219	263	461	337	798
Parcel Post estimate	6	7	13	22	24	46	60	82	95	177
Goods	219	344	563	675	959	1,634	2,196	1,720	2,429	4,149
Coal	-	3	3	7	8	15	17	19	22	41
Other than coal	9	7	16	10	13	23	40	24	50	74
Livestock	41	61	102	62	44	106	208	436	343	779
Sundries	1	2	3	-	-	-	3	-	-	-
TOTAL	673	783	1,456	1,422	1,562	2,985	4,441	5,889	5,896	11,785

EXPENDITURE		Summer	Winter	Total	
	Permanent Way & Signal Dept			2,905	
	Traffic expenses	927	1,252	2,179	
	Running expenses	686	946	1,632	
					6,716
DIRECT LOSS					2,275

MAINTENANCE OF ROLLING STOCK	Summer	Winter	Total	
Locomotives	181	254	435	
Carriages	39	57	96	
Wagons	36	50	86	
TOTAL	256	361	617	
Superintendence			356	
Rates			210	1,183
TOTAL LOSS				3,458

PERMANENT WAY	Length of all track including sidings				28 miles, 1,201 yards	
	Estimated remaining life of the track				3-6 years	
	Value of recovered materials if track lifted				£12,249	
	Estimated cost of recovering materials				£5,736	
	Estimated net value of recovered materials				£6,513	
	Estimated present annual cost of maintenance:					
	Manning line, wages,				£1,940	
	Materials				£437	
	Permanent way saving on closing of branch				£2,377	

TRAFFIC MILEAGE			Summer	Winter	Total
	Train miles	Passenger	11,637	16,101	27,738
		Goods	3,504	4,816	8,320
		Total	15,141	20,917	36,058
	Engine miles	Total	16,189	22,357	38,546

A footnote to this table added, 'N.B. Receipts for Mails not included. On this branch the trains work through from Athlone and the estimated expenditure shown under the heading of Maintenance of Rolling Stock may not be fully saved if the Branch is closed'.

This raises some interesting issues. If the total loss shown for the line, taking everything into account, was £3,458, by how much would this have reduced if income from carriage of mails *had* been included? When the line did eventually close, none of the locomotives used on the line were directly withdrawn - they all went on to be used elsewhere on the system. The same was true of carriage stock, therefore it could have been argued that it was unfair to cost the entire maintenance costs of these to the Achill line. Total maintenance costs were quoted as £617 per year - a simple stroke of the pen would have improved the line's balance sheet by allocating these costs elsewhere.

Having said that, the overall loss would merely have been reduced by these measures, not eliminated, let alone turned round. The line was simply not carrying enough traffic all year round to ensure its financial viability - and there was the matter of the worn-out track to contend with.

In order to evaluate the extent of bus services, which would be needed in lieu of the passenger train service, the following figures were prepared in 1933:

Return of typical Passenger Traffic - Trains from Westport to Achill

Number of passengers leaving Westport*

Train	Week ended 9.7.1932		Week ended 6.8.1932		Week ended 10.9.1932		Week ended 29.10.1932		Week ended 2.1.1933		Week ended 11.3.1933	
	1.00 pm	8.24 pm	1.00 pm	8.24 pm	1.00 pm	8.24 pm	1.00 pm	8.24 pm	1.00 pm	8.24 pm	1.00 pm	8.24 pm
Mon	6	5	16	22	8	7	2	9	3	10	3	10
Tues	5	10	11	29	5	20	6	10	4	12	7	12
Wed	4	9	8	10	10	8	3	8	2	5	4	10
Thurs	14	50	16	58	13	45	3	10	5	10	7	29
Fri	6	11	11	27	5	27	4	6	5	9	5	12
Sat	10	42	11	73	9	33	6	86	3	8	4	22

* The majority of these passengers were for Newport, with smaller numbers for Mallaranny and Achill.

Number of passengers leaving Newport*

Train	Week ended 9.7.1932		Week ended 6.8.1932		Week ended 10.9.1932		Week ended 29.10.1932		Week ended 2.1.1933		Week ended 11.3.1933	
	11.40 am	3.30 pm	11.40 am	3.30 pm	11.40 am	3.30 pm	11.40 am	3.30 pm	11.40 am	3.30 pm	11.40 am	3.30 pm
Mon	24	6	37	12	7	6	9	3	9	11	6	4
Tues	14	4	18	4	24	3	5	4	10	3	1	3
Wed	9	3	7	4	9	6	2	3	10	5	3	3
Thurs	45	13	24	3	25	0	9	6	12	4	18	8
Fri	11	4	26	4	17	4	5	3	3	5	14	3
Sat	18	10	34	18	36	16	12	20	10	10	15	10

*   The majority of these passengers were travelling from Newport to Westport or beyond, with comparatively few having come from Achill or Mallaranny.

It will be noted that the 11.40 am to Westport carried more passengers than the 3.30 pm, and that the 8.24 pm to Achill carried more passengers in the opposite direction. In winter months, numbers rarely exceeded 10 on any train. In summer, the slightly higher numbers can partly be attributed to tourists, though it is obvious that the vast majority of tourists were coming to the area by some means other than the train. The other factor swelling some, but not all, of the summer workings would be the migrating farm workers. On 29th October, the 8.24 pm to Achill carried 86 people - far in excess of the normal pattern. These would be farm workers on the final leg of their long journey from the North Wall quays, Dublin. At off peak times, the passengers could often have required nothing more than a taxi, let alone a bus: for example, on all of the days sampled, not one service on any Wednesday managed to attract more than 10 passengers, and most were less than that. One Westport-bound train on 10th September, 1932 failed to carry a single passenger.

The destinations of travellers on the line tell a story typical of many lines built under the Balfour Act. It was said when they opened that they would develop the areas they served, but once open it was clear that far from encouraging new development in poor areas, they merely made the journey of the emigrant easier. Analysis of passenger returns in the late 1920s and early 1930s shows a significant number of travellers who were not only going beyond the Achill line, but beyond Ireland: this reflected ticket sales through to ports in England or Scotland. Some of this would relate to temporary migrant workers, some to people who were leaving Ireland for good, in search of a wealthier life elsewhere. Much income also related to travellers to and from Dublin.

Goods traffic was also monitored. A table of tonnages relating to the financial year 1932/1933 showed that the average daily tonnage of goods handled at each of the three stations varied considerably. Overall, while Newport was shown above to be the busiest station for passenger traffic, Achill was the busiest for goods traffic, handling 54 per cent of all goods on the line. Achill accounted for 75 per cent of all goods inwards, but Newport loaded 70 per cent of all goods outwards. While Newport had a daily average of four tons being dispatched by train, a maximum amount of 90 tons had occurred on one day - this tonnage being nearly double Achill's largest daily figure. It was considered that a lorry making several runs could cope with this maximum, which was said to be very occasional, and consisted of millstuffs. Cement also played a part in Newport's traffic, this being exported by ship from the harbour there. Mallaranny's goods traffic in both directions was very light, accounting for well under one wagon load per day. The bulk of outgoing traffic from Achill had in earlier years been fish, eggs and agricultural produce, but by this time was turf.

Once lorries were introduced, Achill, Mallaranny and Newport goods sheds became road freight depots.

	Goods In Tons	Goods Out Tons	Approx. daily average Inwards	Outwards	Daily maximum Inwards	Outwards
Newport	933	1,263	3	4	13	90
Mallaranny	683	54	2	0.25	10	6
Achill	3,274	172	11	0.75	50	20
Total	4,890	1,489	16	5		

The only other traffic not included above was cattle. Fairs were held at all three stations on the line, and in the same period the summary of animals dispatched was:

Newport	378 sheep, 284 cattle
Mallaranny	110 cattle
Achill	345 pigs, 56 cattle

Here, Newport was the busiest location again. Not surprisingly, the maximum number handled in a single day was from here - 95 cattle and 328 sheep from one fair day!

The major part of the case that was made by the GSR was that in order to keep the line open some £45,145, or approximately £1,700 per mile, would have to be spent to bring the line into insurable condition. The bulk of this would be spent on track relaying. In 1930, the GSR estimated that the track had about 3-6 years of useful life. By January 1933, an internal report stated that the track had only 6-12 months of useful life left, and cost estimates were prepared showing that the following expenditure would be necessary:

Year 1	£11,999	Year 4	£11,999
Year 2	£4,244	Year 5	£5,729
Year 3	£11,174		

If this were to be costed against traffic receipts on the line over a five-year period, substantial losses would ensue. It was noted that the track from Mallaranny to Achill was in a worse state of repair than Mallaranny-Westport. By November, a further report had shifted its emphasis to calculating the scrap value of the track following closure and dismantling. This report read as follows:

Westport and Achill Branch

	£	£	£
Estimated Capital Cost of proposed Road Services, Equipment and accommodation.			5,285
Estimated Value of Recoverable Materials from the lifting of this Line at present prices:			
Recoverable Materials (a)	12,546		
Scrap Materials (b)	4,169		
Total Estimated Gross Value of recoverable materials		16,715	
Less: Cost of lifting:			
Recoverable Materials (a)	2,648		
Scrap Materials (b)	3,073		
		5,721	
Estimated Net Value of Recoverable Materials -			10,994
Estimated Expenditure over the next five years to put the Permanent Way on this Branch into good working order.			45,145
Proportion of this Expenditure due to be incurred in the first year (1934).			11,999
Estimated annual operating costs of proposed new Road Service, excluding Pensions.			6,020
Estimated existing Railway Expenditure on this Branch based on figures taken out for year ended_____ .			7,568

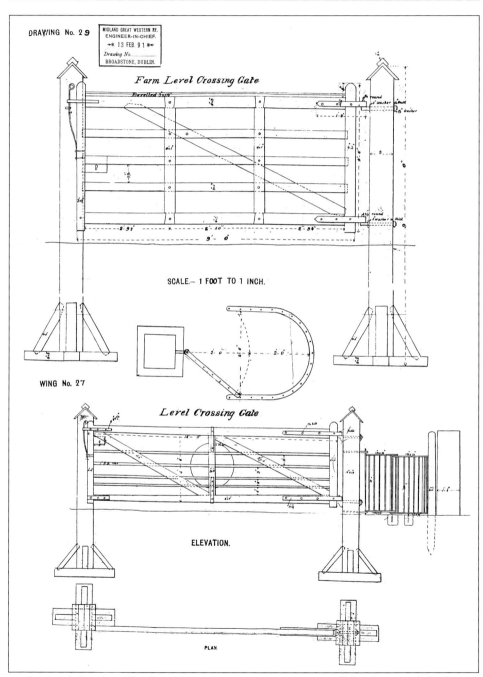

Engineer's drawing of level crossing gate.

H.C.A. Beaumont Collection

Appendix Three

Level Crossings and Bridges

None of the crossings on the Achill line were interlocked with the signalling system, therefore a crossing keeper was stationed at each of the busier ones with a cottage of a standard design provided. The keeper had to keep the oil lamps on the gates lit, and open and close them for traffic. Originally, they were kept shut across the road, rather than the railway, and opened for road traffic. One can only imagine the delays that a system such as this would cause to modern road traffic!

The crossings were as follows:

Milepost	*Name of Crossing*	*Station to which attached*	*Distance from Westport*		*Whether Signalled, and direction*
			Miles	*Yards*	
161¾	Deerpark East	Westport	0	1,570	No
162¼	Attireesh	Westport	1	639	No
164¼	Cross	Westport	3	578	No
164¼	Buckfield	Westport	3	785	Up
165¼	Clooneen	Newport	4	820	Up
165¾	Kilmeena or Knockaboley	Newport	4	1,630	Both
166¼	Gortawarla	Newport	5	740	No
166¾	Corragaun	Newport	5	1,264	Both
171¼	Doontrusk	Newport	10	668	Both
171¾	Derrycooldrim	Newport	10	1,745	Up
173½	Knockbreaga	Newport	12	1,040	No
174¼	Roskeen	Mallaranny	13	703	Up
177¼	Rosturk Crossing	Mallaranny	16	660	No
183¾	Tonregee East	Achill	22	1,492	No
184¾	Tonregee West	Achill	23	1,363	No
186¾	Pollranny	Achill	25	1,466	No

The last railway employees on the Achill line were the crossing gatekeepers at Clooneen, Knockbreaga and Doontrusk, whose services were retained until 23rd October, 1937. After that, they were pensioned off - receiving 12*s*. per week until their 70th birthdays, after which 6*s*. per week was to be paid.

The major bridges and the two tunnels were as follows:

Milepost	*Description*
	Westport station and viaduct
168¼	Tunnel - 88 yards, built to avoid the adjacent sharp curve, the 'deviation'.
168½	Tunnel -133 yards long. These two were the only tunnels on the entire MGWR system.
168¾	Newport viaduct
168¾	Newport station and road overbridge
	Burrishoole Channel bridge
	Furnace Lough road bridge
172½	Carrowsallagh bridge - stopping place for petrol railcar 1911-1916
	Owengarve river bridge
	Glenthomas river bridge
	Bunnahowna river bridge
178¼	Highest point on the line
178¾	Mallaranny Ballast Pit
179¼	Site of temporary Mallaranny station 1894-5
179½	Mallaranny station
	Ballycroy Road bridge
184¾	Tonregee Fish Siding
187½	Achill station

Typical accommodation gate on the Achill line, near Newport. These gates were provided where the line crossed farmland, to enable farmers to reach their land on the other side of the track. In this example, the track ran from left to right in the immediate foreground.   *Author*

Typical gatekeeper's cottage, Achill line. In this case, the level crossing was just to the right of the house, and the gates were roughly where the white wall is now. Many of these houses are still occupied.   *Author*

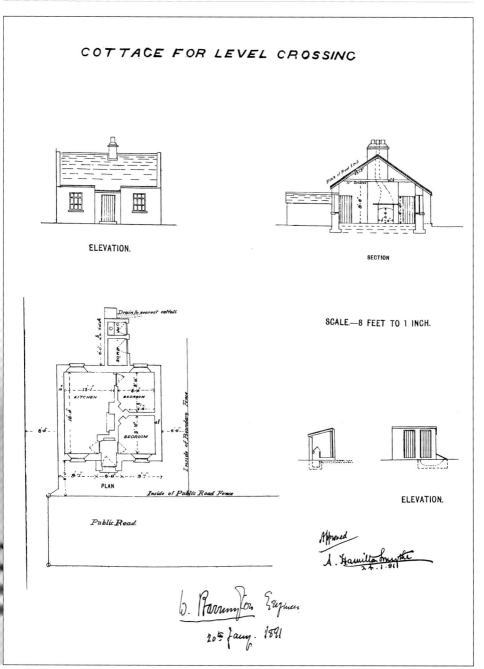

Plans for level crossing gatekeeper's cottage of standard type on the line, signed by the Engineer, William Barrington.

H.C.A. Beaumont Collection

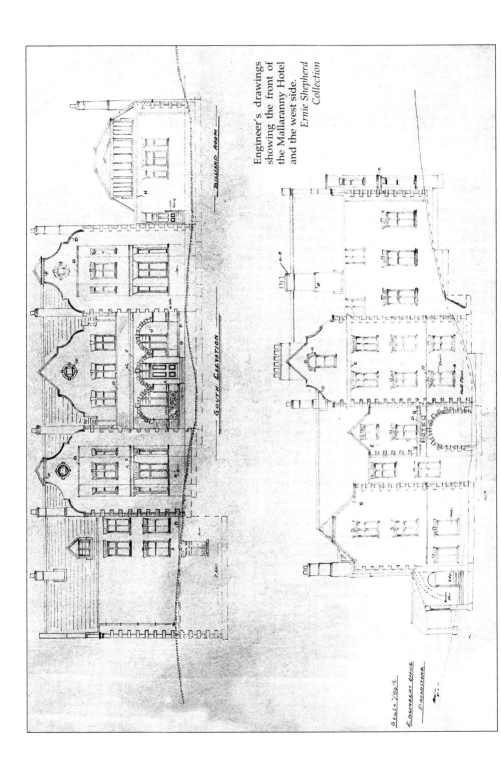

Engineer's drawings showing the front of the Mallaranny Hotel and the west side.
Ernie Shepherd Collection

Appendix Four

Tourism and the Mallaranny Hotel

From planning stage, the Midland Great Western Railway had high hopes for the development of tourist traffic on the railway. A site at Achill Sound was under consideration while the line was still being built, but the site available there was not considered suitable. The first mention of Mallaranny as a potential site for a hotel was in October 1892 when Mr R. Vesey Stoney asked the railway company for a grant of £700-£800 to help him convert a house there into a hotel. The company declined his request, and renewed its examination of a site at Achill. Two years later Vesey Stoney offered to lease a house, Ennell Lodge, on his land adjacent to the railway in Mallaranny, along with '4,000 acres of Shooting'. The company expressed interest, and an offer was made to lease the house plus 20 acres to the company for £50 per year. The company's Engineer surveyed the house and grounds, following which Vesey Stoney was asked to sell it to the company. He agreed, and some negotiation regarding the price followed - Vesey Stoney said he would sell it for £2,000, which the MGWR declined as 'exorbitant'. In the meantime, the Achill Mission in Dugort, Achill Island, offered to rent a field to the company if it built its hotel on the island. The company agreed to this at the time, but nothing further was done.

By February 1895, Vesey Stoney had dropped his asking price to £1,500. The company investigated the site, and the Engineer suggested that Ennell Lodge could be enlarged into a small hotel with 12 guest's rooms and four sitting rooms. The cost was not to exceed £5,000. A water supply would be taken from a lake above the village. According to the engineer, the water in it was 'dark coloured but appears to be used for drinking purposes by the people of the village'. He continued by saying that sewerage could be let run straight into the sea, as there were no houses in the way!

There was an existing hotel on the island, which was to the forefront of the fledgling tourism business in the area. This was the Slievemore Hotel at Dugort, owned by a John Sheridan. In June 1895 the company commenced paying an annual subsidy to Sheridan to operate a coach service between his hotel and the railway station at Achill. This was to continue on and off for many years.

By now, plans had been drawn up for a hotel in Mallaranny. Tenders were submitted, with Worthington (who had constructed the railway) offering to build it for £7,500. A rival bid, by Collens, was successful, and he was offered the contract for £7,498 15s. 11d. Collens' foreman requested that he be allowed to move into Ennell Lodge immediately, as his headquarters and home, but this was declined! By June 1896, work had commenced, but was hampered by bad weather. Arrangements were now being made for a variety of things - a suitable housekeeper was interviewed, a monogram was designed for the linen napkins, and work was in progress installing lifts and kitchen equipment. It was planned to open the hotel on 1st September. Work dragged on, with delays in the installation of the plumbing through the summer. The September deadline was missed, and it was not until March 1897 that a deputation of the company's Directors made a final inspection of the building. They were satisfied, but almost as an afterthought decided to seek estimates for provision of electric lighting. This was arranged hurriedly, with a Mr Norman Robinson agreeing to install electricity for £450.

A Manageress and two caretakers were appointed in mid-March 1897, and the hotel opened for business on the 31st March, a licence to sell alcoholic drinks having been issued on that day. It was named 'The Railway Hotel, Mallaranny'. A total of 104 visitors had stayed in the hotel by mid-July, and new visitors were arriving at the rate of 16-35 per week. After the summer was over, this figure started to fall dramatically, and by November an average of just four per week were staying.

147

Railway Hotel, Mallaranny. This attractive view of the front of the hotel was taken within the first two years of its life, before it was extended in 1899.

Laurence Collection, courtesy National Library of Ireland

In June 1898, a hotel guest named Fottrell alighted from the 9.15 train to stay in the hotel. The unfortunate guest must have found the fresh air to be too much for him, as he died in his bed. Mirroring the railway line, the hotel had had a death around its opening time. Some years later, on 19th January, 1912, the Chairman of the MGWR, Hon. R.A. Nugent, also died in the hotel. He had been a frequent visitor, and the Mallaranny station master, Mr Forbes, was a long standing friend of his. He had been with the company for 25 years, and had been Chairman for the last eight.

Plans were soon being made to improve the hotel. In July 1898, plans were made to build 'hot and cold water seawater baths' at a cost of £500. A causeway was built from across the road in front of the hotel down to the sea, to enable hotel guests to take a walk to the beach. The causeway was 8 feet wide, designed for 'the passage of one car'. It is not clear how a horse-drawn car was meant to negotiate the steps at the inland end of the path!

By 1899, the hotel was being extended. Two workmen fell off scaffolding during the work and were awarded £1 1s. each in compensation. As a result of the extension, 84 guests per week were arriving by July 1899. The causeway was completed by December 1899. By New Year's Eve, there were but three guests, but a request by a local doctor for a dance to be held was turned down!

In the summer season of 1900, a boat was provided for hotel guests to hire for 1s. per hour. In addition, guests had transport provided for short distances by hotel staff, and a shed was provided to accommodate two horses and carts.

By 1901, the company had provided a 9-hole golf course close to the hotel for the use of guests. Advertising matters occupied the railway company's corporate mind, and the manageress was asked to state how many guests had arrived at the hotel as a direct result of a newspaper advertisement. In 1902, consideration was given to employing a member of staff who was able to speak French - Mallaranny was now firmly on the tourist map. In 1902, guest numbers were boosted at the height of the summer by the Achill connection off the Dublin - Galway 'Tourist Express'. This was deemed to be a success and was repeated for the next few years. However, while business was brisk in the summer, the winter months were still not managing to attract more than single figures of guests per week. Miss Kilsby, the Manageress, was told in September 1904 that 'some changes would have to be made'. The hotel was to close during the lean months in the future.

In 1906 a cow was purchased for the hotel, to provide fresh milk.

By 1907 the golf course had been extended. An unusual incident concerned some hotel guests who were members of a golfing party. It was reported that while playing on the golf links owned by the company, they were 'interfered with' by the caretaker. No other details survive, except that the course caretaker was dismissed six months afterwards!

By 1908, the Tourist Express was not the only train service which was operating for the benefit of the hotel. The company ran a train from Achill to Mallaranny and back for the benefit of guests, and to allow Achill people to attend functions in the hotel. This train left Achill at 6.35 pm on two days per week, and returned later in the evening. The following year saw the start of the line's only regular Sunday service ever, to bring worshippers to Newport where the nearest churches were. A big advertising campaign was launched, with hotel posters being put up at every station on the Midland Great Western system.

In 1912, a Ford Car was purchased for the hotel. This was used to ferry guests, luggage, and supplies over short distances. In 1914, a new car was provided at a cost of £380 - the poor roads in the area had obviously inflicted severe wear and tear on the first one. The new car was to be hired to hotel guests at 1s. per mile.

By 1915, it was considered that the savings made in closing the hotel each winter were insignificant. Consequently, it remained open that winter, and the next. Over the next 12 months, a new 'motor entrance' was made between the station and the hotel, and the hotel's hen runs were cleaned up! In May 1920, the wall of the station fell into the Hotel's vegetable garden destroying vegetables and greenhouses. The cause of this mishap was put down to vibration from trains.

Railway Hotel, Mallaranny, soon after opening; Edwardian splendour in the coffee room.

Lawrence Collection, courtesy National Library of Ireland

Midland Great Western Railway.

RAILWAY CO.'S HOTEL AT

MALLARANNY (ACHILL)

Combined Rail and Hotel Tickets

ARE ISSUED AS UNDER FROM 1st APRIL TILL 30th SEPTEMBER.

FROM	FIRST CLASS			THIRD CLASS		
	(a) Weekly Tickets (7 days)	(b) Three-day Tickets	(c) Two-day Tickets	(a) Weekly Tickets (7 days)	(b) Three-day Tickets	(c) Two-day Tickets
	£ s. d.	£ s. d.	£ s. d.	£ s. d.	£ s. d.	£ s. d.
BROADSTONE ...	7 7 0	4 17 0	4 2 0	6 18 0	4 0 0	3 5 0
MULLINGAR ...	7 7 0	4 1 0	3 6 0	6 18 0	3 11 0	2 16 0
ATHLONE ...	7 3 0	3 13 0	2 18 0	6 12 0	3 6 0	2 11 0
ATHENRY ...	7 7 0	4 3 0	3 8 0	6 18 0	3 12 0	2 17 0
GALWAY ...	7 7 0	4 7 0	3 12 0	6 18 0	3 15 0	3 0 0
ROSCOMMON ...	6 16 0	3 9 0	2 14 0	6 7 0	3 2 0	2 7 0
CASTLEREA ...	6 10 0	3 4 0	2 9 0	6 3 0	2 19 0	2 4 0
BALLYHAUNIS ...	6 7 0	3 1 0	2 6 0	5 19 0	2 16 0	2 2 0
CLAREMORRIS ...	6 2 0	2 18 0	2 6 0	5 17 0	2 13 0	2 2 0
CASTLEBAR ...	5 16 0	2 14 0	2 6 0	5 11 0	2 9 0	1 17 0
WESTPORT ...	5 12 0	2 10 0	2 2 0	5 7 0	2 5 0	1 17 0
BALLINA ...	6 5 0	3 1 0	2 6 0	6 0 0	2 16 0	2 2 0
CAVAN ...	7 7 0	4 17 0	—	6 18 0	4 0 0	—

(a) Hotel Accommodation, viz. :—Dinner on day of issue; Breakfast, Lunch, and Dinner on six following days, and Breakfast and Lunch on eighth day; Attendance and Bedroom on seven nights.

(b) Hotel Accommodation, viz. :—Dinner on day of issue; Breakfast, Lunch, and Dinner on two following days; Breakfast and Lunch on third following day; Attendance and Bedroom on three nights.

(c) Hotel Accommodation, viz. :—Dinner on day of issue; Breakfast, Lunch, and Dinner on following day; Breakfast and Lunch on second following day; Bedroom and Attendance on two nights.

Holders of these Tickets must show the Hotel Coupon on entering the Hotel. **Free Fishing,** Golfing and Shooting in connection with above Hotel.

Motor Cars attached to Hotel Garage.

For further particulars apply to the Manageress, Railway Hotel, Mallaranny, Co. Mayo; to Station Masters at the various Stations; or to Traffic Manager, Broadstone, Dublin.

M. F. KEOGH,

General Manager.

BROADSTONE, DUBLIN,
March, 1922.

Browne & Nolan, Ltd., Printers, Dublin.

Achill, Mallaranny, Westport and Clifden.

Tour No. 129

Rail ...	...To Holyhead via Rugby, Nuneaton, Stafford and Chester, *or* via Rugby, Coventry, Birmingham, and Chester.
Steamer	...Holyhead to Kingstown (Dun Laoghaire).
Rail ...	...Kingstown (Dun Laoghaire) to Dublin (Westland Row).
Rail ...	...Dublin (Broadstone) to Achill.
Rail ...	...Achill to Mallaranny.
*Road Motor	...Mallaranny to Clifden.
Rail ...	...Clifden to Dublin (Broadstone).
Rail ...	...Dublin (Westland Row) to Kingstown (Dun Laoghaire)..
Steamer	...Kingstown (Dun Laoghaire) to Holyhead.
Rail ...	...Holyhead to starting point, via Chester.

FARES.

From		1st Class Saloon. s. d.	3rd Class Saloon. s. d.	3rd Class Rail and Steamer. s. d.
London (Euston)	...	189 0	133 9	120 0
„ Liverpool	... ...	117 9	91 0	85 6
„ Birmingham	... ...	147 9	109 0	95 3
„ Manchester	... ...	131 6	99 3	85 6
„ Derby ...	... ...	145 3	107 6	93 9
„ Dudley ...	... ...	144 3	107 0	93 3
„ Leamington	... ...	154 6	113 0	99 3
„ Leeds ...	... ...	145 3	107 6	93 9
„ Leicester	... ...	155 9	114 0	100 3
„ Nottingham	... ...	150 0	110 3	96 6
„ Oxford	... ...	174 0	125 0	111 3
„ Sheffield ...	... ...	144 6	107 3	93 6
„ Wolverhampton	...	142 0	105 9	92 0

* Service operates from June 1st to Sept. 9th.
This tour may be performed in the reverse direction.

Tour No. 130

Rail ...	... To Holyhead.
Steamer	... Holyhead to Kingstown (Dun Laoghaire).
Rail ...	... Kingstown (Dun Laoghaire) to Dublin (Westland Row).
Rail ...	... Dublin (Broadstone) to Achill, via Athlone.
Rail ...	... Achill to Mallaranny.
*Road Motor ...	Mallaranny to Clifden.
Rail ...	... Clifden to Killarney, via Galway, Athenry, & Limerick.
†Road Motor ...	Killarney to Bantry, via Glengarriff.
Rail ...	... Bantry to Cork.
Rail ...	... Cork to Wexford, via Lismore and Waterford.
Rail ...	... Wexford to Rosslare Harbour.
Steamer	... Rosslare Harbour to Fishguard.
Rail ...	... Fishguard to starting point.

FARES.

From		1st Class Saloon. s. d.	3rd Class Saloon. s. d.	3rd Class Rail and Steamer. s. d.
London ...	... ...	245 3	165 3	151 6
„ Birmingham	... ...	236 0	159 9	146 0

* Service operates from June 1st to Sept. 9th.
† Service operates from June 1st to Sept. 30th.
This tour may be performed in the reverse direction.

Passengers may travel by the Road Motor from Glengarriff *to Macroom*, thence rail to Cork, instead of Road Motor Glengarriff *to* Bantry, thence Rail to Cork.

Service operates from June 1st to Sept. 30th only.

Extract from the LMS *Programme of Circular Tours in Great Britain in England, Scotland, Ireland and Wales*, 1933.

The political unrest of this period affected the hotel, which was occupied by the Irregulars between April and December 1922, while the Free State forces were in it during 1923. Between the two of them, they inflicted much damage on the hotel and it took almost the whole of 1924 to put matters to right. A military report of the time claimed that the Irregulars based in the Mallaranny / Ballycroy area were in possession of two to three armoured cars, 'made out of Boilers taken from MALRANNY HOTEL', along with a 'Flying Column' of five lorries, 116 cyclists, and a quantity of arms and ammunition. This local force was considered by the Free State forces to be the most impenetrable in the area, and they had to request further arms and equipment from Dublin to deal with it.

From January 1925, the MGWR became part of the Great Southern Railways and the hotel was renamed the Great Southern Hotel, part of a group of former railway hotels in its ownership. The GSR carried out some improvements over the next two years, but in 1934 embarked on a major refurbishment programme. A new car, another Ford, was purchased for £225, and a 'Wireless Radiogram' was provided to keep hotel guests in touch with the world.

When the line closed in 1937, the GSR decided to keep the hotel. Few guests were arriving by train by this stage, as tourists had taken to the roads in the area. The GSR made arrangements for a bus to be available to carry guests if necessary, but it was considered that the replacement public bus service would be adequate. The old station building remained in GSR ownership, and was used eventually as hotel staff quarters and storage space. Only the signal cabin was demolished. The hotel was still in railway ownership when the GSR itself was absorbed into Coras Iompair Eireann in 1945. CIE was nationalised in 1950, and all the Great Southern Hotel chain was placed under the administration of its hotel subsidiary, OIE. By this stage, tourist patterns were beginning to change, as more and more holidaymakers began to travel abroad. Losses mounted, and by the 1970s the hotel was no longer trading profitably. Few guests were staying at all, and most of the business came from the bar, wedding and business functions, and the restaurant. In 1977, CIE sold the hotel into private ownership. As a privately owned concern again, but having severed its railway parentage, the hotel continued as the Great Western Hotel, and later the Mulrany Bay Hotel. Several changes of ownership could not bring the good days back, and in 1991 the hotel shut its doors for good. At the time of writing, it has lain derelict for over 10 years, despite several attempts to re-open it.

The hotel building is a fine structure, which dominates the skyline above Mulrany village. It is to be hoped that some permanent use can be found for it.

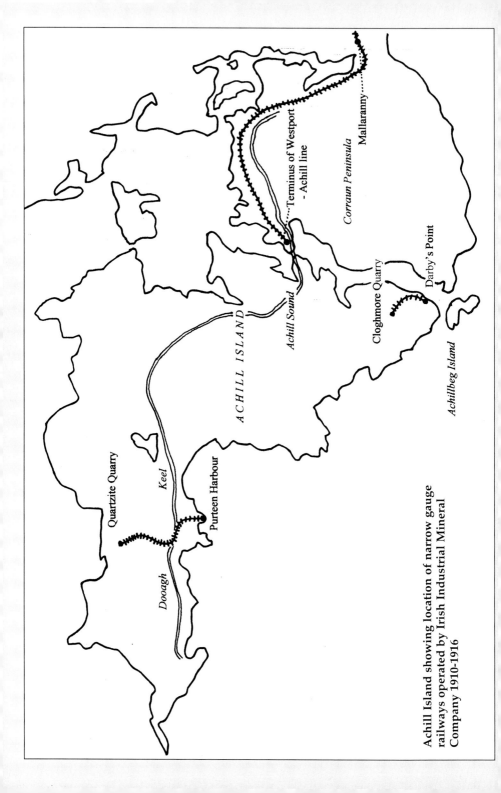

Achill Island showing location of narrow gauge railways operated by Irish Industrial Mineral Company 1910-1916

Appendix Five

Achill Mineral Railways

While the Achill line itself stopped on the mainland side of the bridge, Achill Island itself was not without its own railways. The Irish Industrial Mineral Company was involved in excavating rocks at two locations on the island in the 1910s, and a 2 ft gauge railway was laid at each place to carry the rock to nearby piers for loading into boats. The company had been promoted by a local man, but was managed by a Mr Carder, from North Wales.

At Cloghmore, in the south of the island, a short line connected the quarry with the pier at Darby's Point. The line was gravity worked for a mile downhill, with sets generally made up of six wagons descending to sea level. At this point horses hauled the wagons to the pier, where they were offloaded. This line operated from around 1910 for several years, and was broken up in 1920. No trace of the line remains now, although it is believed that the laneway from the road up to the Achill Quartz Quarry follows the route of it.

A more ambitious line operated from a quartz quarry near Keel to the pier at Purteen Harbour. From the harbour, the line ran inland and crossed the road near the Achill Head Hotel, before continuing for about 1½ miles towards the quarry. It gained considerable height over this route, before gradually falling towards the quarry, where a locomotive shed, boiler house and weighbridge were provided. A second locomotive shed was provided at the Keel end (Pollagh), just across the road from the Achill Head Hotel. The line had at least two passing loops or sidings along its route. Wagons were stored here when out of use, and the end one was derailed to prevent them running away. This rudimentary method of preventing accidents did not stand up to the ingenuity of local youths, however. A young boy had to have his legs amputated after being run over by one, and his parents sued the mining company. They argued that the boy was at fault, because either he or his companions had deliberately re-railed the wagon in order to take an illicit trip along the line. The court agreed, and ruled in favour of the company.

A more serious accident occurred shortly after the line opened. The line's first locomotive, *Derwent*, ran away on a severe gradient (of 1 in 10!), and was badly damaged, the chimney being broken off, and the cab destroyed. The driver, a native of Athlone named Curley, was seriously injured, indeed his survival was considered miraculous. Once recovered, he spent a long life in charge of a stationary steam engine in Athlone. This had not been his first accident - before commencing employment with the Irish Industrial Minerals Company, he had been a driver on the MGWR. As a result of injuries received in a collision between the down Night Mail and a line of wagons at Manulla Junction, he had had to be pensioned off by the railway company.

After *Derwent* was damaged, the second engine arrived by boat at Westport Quay in 1912. *Derwent* was subsequently repaired, and both locomotives operated during the remainder of the line's short life.

At full capacity, the quarry employed 100 men. Most of the unskilled jobs were held by local men, but the mining company drafted in some staff, including skilled locomotive men, from outside the area. Two steam locomotives were used to bring 100 tons of stone per day to the pier. It was shipped from there to Westport Quay, where it was processed through grinding machinery, before being shipped to England for use in the manufacture of pottery. This line commenced operations in 1910, but by 1916 the company abandoned the quarry, due to the excessive manpower costs. While wages were low, the cost of taking the raw material to where it was needed was prohibitive. The line lay in limbo, before T.W. Ward of Sheffield bought the entire plant in 1920. The line was entirely dismantled, and both locomotives were taken by boat to England. The course of the line

Right: Derwent - the first locomotive on the Keel line of the Irish Industrial Mineral Company. The location of the photograph is outside one of the two locomotive sheds on the line - either that at Pollagh, opposite the Achill Head hotel, or at the white stone quarry at the upper end of the line. The identities of the man standing by the engine, and the child on the front of it, are unknown.   *Irish Railway Record Society*

Below: King George - the second and bigger locomotive on this line.
                    Irish Railway Record Society

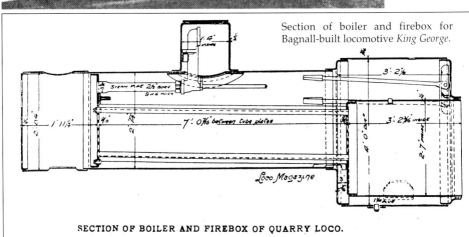

Section of boiler and firebox for Bagnall-built locomotive *King George*.

SECTION OF BOILER AND FIREBOX OF QUARRY LOCO.

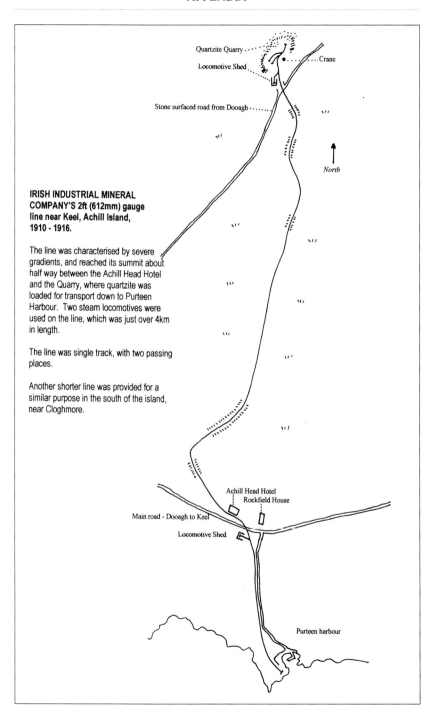

Quartzite Quarry

Locomotive Shed

Crane

Stone surfaced road from Dooagh

North

IRISH INDUSTRIAL MINERAL COMPANY'S 2ft (612mm) gauge line near Keel, Achill Island, 1910 - 1916.

The line was characterised by severe gradients, and reached its summit about half way between the Achill Head Hotel and the Quarry, where quartzite was loaded for transport down to Purteen Harbour. Two steam locomotives were used on the line, which was just over 4km in length.

The line was single track, with two passing places.

Another shorter line was provided for a similar purpose in the south of the island, near Cloghmore.

Achill Head Hotel
Rockfield House

Main road - Dooagh to Keel

Locomotive Shed

Purteen harbour

was clearly visible for some 40 years afterwards, but in more recent times much has been obliterated. However, it is still possible to trace a path where the main line would have run. At the site of the quarry, no trace remains of the locomotive shed and other buildings, but their location is marked by piles of stones. At the Keel end of the line, the locomotive shed is believed to have been incorporated into a house.

Details of the two locomotives have survived. They were as follows:

Locomotive Name	*Derwent*	*King George*
Wheel arrangement	0-4-0T	0-6-0T
Builder	Orenstein & Koppel, Berlin	Bagnall, Stafford, England.
Date built	*c.*1900	1911
Maker's number		1945
Cylinders	6½ in. x 12 in.	9 in. x 14 in.
Firebox	15 sq. ft	20½ sq. ft
Wheelbase	2 ft 4 in.	6 ft 6 in.
Tank capacity	100 gallons	210 gallons
Coal capacity	6 cwt	10 cwt
Weight in working order	6½ tons	12½ tons

Achill Island - one of the remaining stretches of embankment which carried the mineral railway across wild bogland. The scenic beauty of the area is evident - apart from the island itself, the western half of the railway to Achill Sound traversed similar countryside.

Author

Acknowledgements and Bibliography

This publication would not have been possible without the help of many people. I would like to acknowledge the help I received from Peter Rigney and David Carse (Dublin); and Norman McAdams (for arranging access to material held in the archives of the Irish Railway Record Society). Dympna Kelledy of Iarnrod Eireann was instrumental in allowing me access to Iarnrod Eireann's archives, while Paddy O'Brien and Ernie Shepherd were on hand to help me to sift through them. The staff of the Irish National Archives and the National Library in Dublin were most helpful, and thanks are also due to Johnny O'Meara, Charles Friel and Barry Carse of the Railway Preservation Society of Ireland, Frank Dawson (Co. Galway), Ed Murphy (Co. Kildare), the late Eamonn Lacken and the late Bob Clements. I have also received much invaluable assistance from many people in the Newport, Corraun and Achill areas. In particular, I would like to thank Joe Sweeney (Achill Sound) and John O'Shea (Dooagh, Achill Island) for their help with original photographs, maps and information.

Little has been published before relating to the Achill line. As a result, almost all material in this book came from primary sources, most notably the archives of the National Library of Ireland, the National Museum, and Irish Rail. Some articles published in the Journal of the Irish Railway Record Society have been helpful, and a good description of the Achill mineral lines was published in a book entitled *Achill*, by Kenneth McNally (David & Charles). I am indebted also to Padraig O'Cuimin (Co. Galway) who lent me a transcript of a talk he gave to the IRRS on the subject of the Achill line.

There is little surviving photograpic material of the line. The National Library of Ireland holds the negatives of the collection of William Lawrence, who took photographs all over Ireland between 1880 and the 1910s. Extensive use has been made of these and of another collection, that of Henry Casserley. Casserley's name is well known in railway circles - he travelled throughout Ireland in the 1930s photographing the railway system. His collection was kindly made available by his son, Richard Casserley. Apart from Casserley's and Lawrence's photographs, surviving pictures of the Achill line and its trains in action are in single figures - those reproduced in this book represent all that the author could uncover in 12 years of research. The Irish Railway Record Society in Dublin has a selection of photographs of the line which may be viewed by appointment. Most of these are of Casserley origin.

Maker's plate on the side of the road bridge, which spanned the western end of Newport station. This bridge is still extant.   *Author*

Index

Westport station from the exterior, 2001. The architectural similarity with Newport station is evident. *Author*